LIVING IN CHRIST

Living in CHRIST

*Essays on the Christian Life
by an Orthodox Nun*

MOTHER RAPHAELA
(WILKINSON)

ST VLADIMIR'S SEMINARY PRESS
CRESTWOOD, NEW YORK

Library of Congress Cataloging-in-Publication Data

Raphaela, Mother.
   Living in Christ: essays on the Christian life by an
Orthodox nun / Mother Raphaela (Wilkinson).
      p. cm.
   Includes bibliographical references.
   ISBN 0-88141-199-x
      1. Christian life—Orthodox Eastern authors.
      I. Title.

BX382 .R35 20000
248.4'819—dc21   99-088452

ST VLADIMIR'S SEMINARY PRESS

575 Scarsdale Road
Crestwood, New York, 10707
www.svspress.com
1-800-204-2665

ISBN 0-88141-199-x
ISBN 978-0-88141-199-7

Contents

Introduction

A new thing is happening in North American Orthodoxy. For the first time in history there is a significant movement of men and women attempting to live the monastic life within the Orthodox Church on this continent. At least sixty monastic or quasi-monastic communities have sprung up in recent years, most of them consisting of four or five members. Most of these places were started and remain governed by monastic elders from abroad. The Holy Myrrhbearers Monastery, whose abbess wrote these essays, is not one of these. This monastery was founded by Mother Raphaela, a former Episcopalian nun, who continues to be its leader and guide.

As a nun in the Episcopal Church, Mother Raphaela taught school, played the organ, edited the community's publication, represented the convent in diocesan committees (such as the task force appointed to discuss the ordination of women), and served as novice mistress of the province. She left the Episcopal Church after more than ten years in monastic life and joined the Orthodox Church in 1977 in the parish where I was then serving as pastor. That same year she was blessed to continue living the monastic life in the Orthodox Church in America with another former Episcopalian sister. The Community of the Holy Myrrhbearers was soon established. In 1983 it acquired its present property, and in 1997 it was named a monastery by His Beatitude Metropolitan Theodosius with Mother Raphaela installed as its abbess, at the Metropolitan's request, by Bishop Seraphim of Ottawa.

Over the last twenty years Mother Raphaela has written essays on the Christian life in her community newsletter as well as for other Church publications. These reflections, some of which are published in this little book, were born and shaped by her interactions with the women who came to test their monastic vocations, with the seekers who spent time in the monastic setting, with Mother's many correspondents, and with the many friends and supporters, as well as questioners and critics, who observe the life and work of the Holy Myrrhbearers Monastery.

These essays are unique not only because of the method of their emergence, but because of the uniqueness of their author. For the very first time in North American Orthodox Church history we have an American-born woman who has lived the monastic life since her teenage years, the last twenty in the Orthodox Church, writing essays on essential elements of Christian living and spiritual striving in the North American context. For this reason alone this book is worth reading.

But it is worth reading, of course, for more than its historical interest. It is worth reading because it testifies first of all to the Orthodox conviction that a person is first and foremost a Christian, a disciple of Christ, a believer in God's gospel concerning Jesus His Son; and can only then be identified as a priest, a layperson, a monk or a nun.

It testifies as well to the conviction that there are not two gospels, or two ways, or two lives, or two truths in the Christian Church; one for those living "in the world" and one for those living in monasteries. There is but one gospel and but one way, life and truth – who is Christ Jesus himself—which can and indeed must be lived in different ways by different people according to their specific callings and conditions provided by the Lord.

And this precious little book also testifies to the conviction, which is an old and venerable conviction of Orthodox Christians, that monastic believers can speak to the rest of us

Christians in very important, significant and meaningful ways, and that they truly must do so for the sake of the soundness and health of God's entire household, the whole body of Christ.

Prayer and silence, faith and obedience, purity and maturity, family and celibacy, building and responsibility, and most especially and most excellently, the way of love, are for every human being. This is the teaching of Christ. And this is the teaching of all Christians, and most surely of those called to the monastic way.

If we ask what a monk or nun can tell the rest of us about life in this fallen, sinful and secularized world, since they live locked and sealed in monastic isolation, we get several answers which we find in this present book. First of all we learn that monks and nuns come from this very world and are still compelled to deal with it on a daily basis, not only around them and over them, but surely within them, in their minds, hearts and bodies; in their memories, emotions and passions. We learn too that the same devils who work in the secular societies and fragile human families work overtime in Christian monasteries and monastic communities. We learn too that the struggles we face "in the world" are faced in monastic enclosure, sometimes with a ferocity and a violence and an inability to be avoided and denied which we "worldlings" cannot even begin to conceive or imagine. And we also learn that we need to hear the voice of the desert, the word of the wilderness, precisely because that setting can provide us with a viewpoint and perspective manifesting a clarity and sharpness that we cannot achieve in the midst of our ceaseless movement, boundless activity and endless clamor and noise.

In a word, the voice from the monastery is relevant for the rest of us precisely because it comes from the monastery. It is precisely its monastic setting which produces its power, guarantees its relevance, and secures its significance for us. Let us

receive it from Mother Raphaela with thanksgiving, as a new
gift from God for our exhortation, edification, encouragement
and enlightenment.

Father Thomas Hopko
St Vladimir's Seminary[1]

---

1 Protopresbyter Thomas Hopko is Dean of St Vladimir's Orthodox Theological Seminary, 575 Scarsdale Road, Crestwood, NY
   10707. He has also been Spiritual Advisor to Holy Myrrhbearers
   Monastery since 1977

1

The Christian Way of Life

"And God saw everything that He had made, and behold, it was very good."[1] "For God so loved the world that He gave his only Son, that whoever believes in Him should not perish but have eternal life."[2]

These two quotes, one from the Old and one from the New Testament, form the basis of Orthodox Christian teaching about our creation and redemption: God made a good world, pure and holy, free from evil, and He delighted in this creation. Though it is deformed by all the evil that has entered in through the fall, God loves it so much that He has redeemed it at a price far beyond what our words can describe. Our faith is life-affirming. It invites us, in the image and likeness of God, to delight in and to enjoy creation and life.

Yet listen: "If any one comes to me and does not hate his own father and mother and wife and children and brothers and sisters, yes, and even his own life, he cannot be my disciple."[3] "If your right eye causes you to sin, pluck it out and throw it away; it is better that you lose one of your members than that your whole body be thrown into hell. And if your right hand causes you to sin, cut it off and throw it away..."[4] "If any man would come after me, let him deny himself and take up his cross daily and follow me."[5] How do we harmonize these hard

1 Genesis 1:31.
2 John 3:16.
3 Luke 14:26.
4 Matthew 5:29-30.
5 Luke 9:23.

sayings by Jesus, who is Himself God and the Son of God, with God's life-affirming delight in creation?

In the Genesis story, even before Adam fell, evil had entered creation in the form of the serpent in the garden of Paradise. The serpent has been identified as Lucifer, the "light bearer," the greatest and most beautiful of the angels, who chose in his God-given freedom not to love God, but rather to envy Him and attempt to create a mode of existence opposed to His reality. The story of the fall of Adam and Eve in the garden of Eden is the story of Lucifer's success in winning others to his side. It tells of the beginning of vicious spiritual warfare.

Thus creation is no longer wholly beautiful and good. Though most of us seem to be born with an innate sense of the goodness of creation, and a desire to enjoy it, we have chosen to side with the forces of destruction and death. Our perceptions and thinking have become warped: that which the Creator of the world and our own common sense have told us is not our business becomes the most important thing for us to hold in our grasp. We take poison, and wonder why we find ourselves sick and dying. We continue to take poison and blame God for the results. We feed poison to those around us and pour it over everything we see. We nourish deep resentments because we cannot use poison and also stay well and healthy in the midst of good and beautiful surroundings.

The reality of life is that we are all born with poison in our system, and we are all born into a poisoned universe. We are unable to hear our God in Christ calling us to use our God-given common sense to see that no matter how pleasant and delightful taking poison may seem to our twisted perceptions and feelings, the results of using poison are clearly insanity, destruction and death.

Through the Church, God in Christ reveals to us the good news that as Man, He has entered His own creation. He Himself has taken on all the effects of the poison, through and beyond the point of death: He has gone into the very depths of hell and broken its power. As God He has raised to life that which was dead through the effects of sin, by being raised from the dead Himself . As Man, He has raised us with Himself, giving us the way back into a sane and holy life in Paradise, set free from the serpent's power.

Jesus very specifically told His disciples in Jerusalem before His Passion that He was going to show them this way; that He himself is the way and that He is life and truth. He did not remove man's freedom: we may still refuse to hear. We may still choose to drink poison and die. Yet we also may use freedom as He intended: to turn to Him, to cry out to Him to show us how to accept His way of reality. We may allow Him to bring us to repentance; we may allow Him to show us how much we ourselves have caused both our own sickness and sickness in all those around us. We may begin to love Him and to speak to Him as to a friend. We may come to see how far we accepted a poisoned relationship with Him, seeing Him and treating Him as less than a person, rather than as the most fully human person in our lives. We may begin to desire to return, to walk in the way of Christ.

Yet we are each at least two people: one, a voice of sanity and common sense calling us to repent of our past thinking and behavior; the other a combination of many voices speaking both from the depths of our own poisoned past and from the poisoned depths around us. The more we try to follow Christ's voice of sanity and common sense, the louder those other voices become, until the devil shows himself as openly powerful and active evil infiltrating even our mind and physical being.

Now the Lord's "hard sayings" begin to make sense to us. "If your hand offends you, cut it off." All things are good before God, yet they can be used in such a poisoned way that we must turn away from them if we are not to be entrapped by deadly contamination. An obvious example is "wine that gladdens the heart of man." Wine is good. It is so good that Christ chose it for His first miracle at the wedding of Cana, and chose it to be His own blood in the Eucharist. For some, however, through the inheritance of a poisoned family life and the effects of their own choices to misuse it, it's effect is so deadly they must cut themselves off completely from its use. To paraphrase the Lord's words, it is better to go dry into paradise, than by drinking to enter into hell.

As hard as it may seem, and as powerless to do it as we may feel ourselves to be, we must ask God for the strength to cut off whatever causes such a craving in us. Only so can we hope to regain it later—even if only in paradise—in a more balanced way. Food, no less than alcohol, is good and to be enjoyed, and we are bound to use it to live. However, to make sure that its use does not gain a destructive control over our lives, we need to practice serious restraint in its use for periods of time. This is a central reason for times of fasting in the Church. The same is true of our relationships with others. Common sense tells us we need family and friends, we need to love and be loved deeply, but when we cannot be near others without trying to figure out how to use them or please them, then love has at best taken second place. We may even need to cut off some relationships so that we can turn to Jesus Christ. He is the one human person who fully knows us and loves us, and with Him we come to know how to be loved and how to love others in return. "If any one comes to Me and does not hate his own father and mother and wife and children and brothers and sisters, yes, and even his own life, he cannot be My disciple."

However, when the devil sees us choosing to free ourselves from his destructive power and turning to follow Christ, he manifests himself much more actively. Serious attempts to live a sane and godly life can bring on terrible suffering, far beyond the voluntary self-denial of those learning to love creation.

Yet those who know God's victory in Jesus over suffering and death do not turn away from this but go forward as Jesus went forward to His crucifixion, in freedom and in joy. They know that with Christ they will come through suffering purified and strong. When physical death comes, they will find they have died only to sin and suffering on earth. They will find the paradise of eternal life, where all that is good, true, pure and holy is present and set free from its poisoned earthly existence. There, when they love God and His creation, there will be no evil to cause suffering. They will be able to delight fully in Him and all He has made simply because of the goodness and beauty that are present. The senseless struggle to try to use creation for purposes it could never fulfill will be ended and replaced by progressive growth through eternity into the infinite love, joy and song of God.

This is the heart of Christian life. This is the heart of our monastic way.

2

Prayer and Life

"That they may have life and have it abundantly."[1] In these words the Lord speaks of what He desires for all of us; indeed of what He desires for the whole of His creation. What means has He given us to gain this life? He has given us the fruits of His own life, passion, death and resurrection. But how do we make these our own? How do we enter into the mystery He offers to us? Simply to go through the motions of receiving Holy Communion is not enough. As St Paul tells us, to eat His Body and drink His Blood unworthily are to eat and drink to our own judgment.[2]

Is it by prayer? Yes, prayer is the only way. But only as we pray in the Lord's own Spirit of truth will our prayer be the doorway to abundant life. There are many artificial forms of prayer that lead us to dead ends. We can get so involved in the external mechanisms of prayer that we lose sight of the goal. It is possible even to worship ideas of prayer and lose the living God in the process.

Prayer is nothing other than bringing our whole self, heart, mind and body, before God,[3] that He may in turn fill us with His own abundant life. This is an effort that takes the whole of our lives and demands everything we can possibly bring to it. We must strive with every ounce of our effort, knowing that when we do so it is God who is working within us.[4] We must train our bodies to worship God and serve our brethren. We must learn to walk in the ways of God-given virtue and morality. And we must learn to use our minds rightly.

1 John 10:10.
2 1 Corinthians 11:27-30.
3 Cf. Matthew 22:37-38.
4 Philippians 2:12-13.

The great saints and fathers of the Church, such as the theologians, St Basil, St Gregory and St John Chrysostom, and their successors, St Gregory Palamas, the great champion of hesychastic prayer, had a solid foundation in secular studies. Moreover, their minds and consciences were trained through the study of the Old and New Testaments, the lives and writings of the saints and the liturgical texts of the Church.

Until very modern times, study meant getting as much "by heart" as possible.[5] Today, television and education may leave us nearly incapable of memorizing words, let alone knowing them so well that we continually ponder them in our hearts.[6] Yet we must learn to do this. The liturgical services of the Church are a great school for this. If we try to participate in them with attention and understanding, we find ourselves disciplining our bodies and immersing our minds and hearts in the Scriptures and hymns of the Church over and over again. We gradually allow our whole being to be filled with God-given truths. The Lord told us: "Out of the fullness of the heart the mouth speaks."[7] More and more, we should be able to speak from these riches rather than out of the poverty of our hearts. We will learn to test our hearts by hearing how busy our mouths are in "normal" conversations with our self-centered thoughts, complaints and wishes rather than with the truth and beauty of God.

St Paul tells us that we must take on the mind of Christ.[8] We cannot fathom the mind of God,[9] yet we can try to learn from the Gospels about the human mind of Jesus. As we study the Gospel

5   See Jean Leclercq, OSB, *The Love of Learning and the Desire For God* (New York: Fordham U. Press. 1974), esp. chapter five: "Sacred Learning."
6   Ibid., and Luke 2:19.
7   Matthew 12:34.
8   1 Corinthians 2:16, Philippians 2:5.
9   1 Corinthians 2:16.

accounts, we will come to see that His was a mind that sought to learn about His faith from an early age.[10] As was His custom, He went regularly to the synagogue and read and interpreted the Scriptures.[11] He lived His entire life as a conscious fulfillment of the history of Israel revealed in those same Scriptures.[12] By the end of His earthly life, He had made the words of the Psalms so much His own that as He was dying on the Cross, they were what came to His lips. "My God, my God, why have You forsaken me?"[13] We must try to do the same.

Even children can be taught simple ways of prayer such as calling on the Lord with a brief phrase like "Lord Jesus Christ, Son of God, have mercy on me a sinner." Only as we are laying a Christ-like foundation of discipline, study and life in the God-given context of the Church, however, can we safely attempt the techniques of using such a phrase in advanced, hesychastic prayer. To try to prematurely quiet the mind and calm the passions and emotions by the incessant use of prayer ropes, breathing techniques, etc., without being grounded in godly study including obedience, can mean serious danger and even mental breakdown. There are times when we need to face our thoughts and emotions and struggle with them, not anesthetize ourselves.

We must bring to all prayer the fullness of the faith of Israel, old and new, with its broad understanding of the God who created and loves the whole universe, and not just our own fallen ideas and opinions. History teaches us that those who attempt advanced techniques before they have reached a certain maturity do not become saints filled with the breadth of the love of the Creator but narrow fanatics. Unfortunately, through the cen-

10 Luke 2:46-47.
11 Luke 4:16.
12 Luke 24:27.
13 Matthew 27:46.

turies monastics have earned a reputation for such narrow fanaticism as often as they have been known for their true sanctity.[14]

For this reason, we have to be careful that we do not debase the ways of prayer that are available to us as Orthodox Christians. It is not only followers of exotic "eastern" cults who seem to despise or fear the mind and attempt to wipe out thinking and emotion with techniques of meditation such as the constant repetition of words or phrases called "mantras." There are also Orthodox who seem to encourage prayer in a language people do not speak or understand, and tell people uneducated in the faith to use the Jesus prayer in place of the services of the Church in ways that come uncomfortably close to the misuse of mantras.

Even St Anthony the Great and St Pachomius, two great founders of monasticism, who did not have backgrounds in secular learning, insisted on the necessity of study. St Anthony, who could not read, based his whole life on the impact of the Scripture readings he heard and memorized by attending Church from the time he was a young child.[15] Pachomius insisted that his monks be taught to read and that they spend every possible free moment memorizing the Scriptures; the Psalms and the entire New Testament were the required minimum.[16] They were to recite these as they worked, walked, etc.,[17] as modern monastics might recite the Jesus prayer.

Through the ages the specific disciplines and schools of

14 History even records cases of monks forming violent mobs. See, for example, John Meyendorff's *Imperial Unity and Christian Divisions: The Church, 450-680 AD* (Crestwood, NY: St Vladimir's Seminary Press, 1989), 185-186.

15 St Athanasius, *The Life of Anthony*, trans. Robert C. Gregg (Classics of Western Spirituality Series, New York: Paulist Press, 1980), sections 1-3.

16 St Pachomius, Precept 140 in *Pachomian Koinonia,* Vol. 2 (Kalamazoo, MI: Cistercian Publications, 1981).

17 Ibid., Precepts 13, 28, 37, 59, 60, 116 and 121.

prayer change and grow in order to lead men and women to the unchanging truths of God in human contexts altered sometimes drastically by the ravages of history. Although the training in prayer may not have changed over the centuries on the Holy Mountain, for example, the men who go there and are trained have changed. When St Gregory Palamas was writing in defense of the hesychasts, even illiterate peasants who became monks were still speaking a language nearly identical to the language they heard in Church. They would arrive having spent many, many hours from infancy in Church, hearing and understanding the words of the services including the Psalms and other readings from the Old and New Testaments. Such illiterate peasants were far ahead of many modern people "educated" in the secular sense, for they could memorize naturally and easily.

Today, many of those who go to monasteries have barely understood a word in Church, nor have they been taught the Scriptures. Rather, their minds are filled with the chaos of a modern, idolatrous and materialistic culture, brainwashed by television and the incessant noise of radios and tape recorders. Many of them are functionally illiterate, and find reading and study exhausting. They cannot listen to and retain what they hear unless it is presented as entertainment. Their minds seem to be atrophied, unable to think creatively, repeating only the opinions and commercials fed to their brains by modern media or their current guru. They need a long period of remedial training, building a foundation in the faith and life of the Church before they can safely embark on the building of hesychastic prayer.

Misuse of the prayer and devotion of the Church are rightly rejected by those who want to follow in the footsteps of Jesus. With the Psalmist, they want to cry: "How manifold are Your works, O Lord! In wisdom have You made them all!"[18] With

18 Psalm 104:24.

St Anthony, they want to read the book of created things:[19] the beauty of places; the grandeur of the desert.[20] They want abundant life, not boxed religion. They want to call on the Lord in the context of this abundant life, which is His own. Any forms of prayer they use will be the means to this end; nothing more, nothing less.

19 St Anthony, quoted by Evagrius in *Practicus* 92 (Guillaumont, ed.), 694.
20 Athanasius, *Life of Anthony*, sections 49-50.

3

Silence Today

How often we hear parents lamenting that they have no idea what is going on with their teenagers: "He (or she) just won't talk!" Or we hear that so-and-so is not speaking to such-and-such because they are offended by them or by their behavior. Conversely, friends working with young people in parish or school situations often share with us their observations that young people seem to have an inability to handle even short periods of silence. Our own experience with women wanting to enter the monastic life confirms these observations. It seems that most people today have encountered silence only as a negative quality—the inability or unwillingness to communicate, or a weapon used to withhold the Word of love, trust and forgiveness that Christians are called to offer to one another, even within families.

It seems to us that there are also two other aspects of this discomfort with silence that compound the problem. Education through television has formed more than a generation into people who cannot use silence. Their experience of learning is not that of struggling to understand. Rather, they are thoroughly conditioned to "learn" only by being entertained; to absorb passively what is explained to them without any exercise of creative thought. Childhood development experts are now claiming that children raised with the television as their baby sitter and primary educator from a pre-school age are unable later to regain the creative learning abilities they normally would have formed during that period of their development.[1] It

1 For example, the following excerpts from articles in *Better Homes and Gardens* magazine, by John Rosemond "a family psy-

is no wonder that blocks of silent time without "input," not to say entertainment, leave such people at a loss. They do not have the mental equipment to deal with them.

We would like to think that few children are that severely disabled. Yet friends of ours who are educators say that this is not fantasy; that teaching young people today is nearly a hopeless task unless one has high-powered media tools and the talents of a television entertainer. We hope that a therapeutic process will be developed for such a damaged generation, so that even if it involves much hard work as part of their later

chologist, a nationally syndicated columnist, and a regular contributor to BH&G" (Used with permission)

November 1988, p.26. "Taming the TV Monster":

Activity turns on the developmental process. The more a child is engaged in imaginative play during the preschool, or formative years, the more that child will realize his or her potential for well-rounded competence. Television pacifies a child's intellect, imagination, and body. It is an asocial and unrealistic experience tantamount to developmental deprivation. The average preschooler watches 30 hours of TV a week - more time than is spent in unstructured, imaginative play. By age 16, that child will have watched 16,000 hours of TV versus only 12,000 hours spent in school... There is no replacing developmental time once it is lost. An hour spent watching even the best educational programs is an hour better spent outside making mud pies.

But, regardless of the programs being watched, a child should spend no more than five hours a week in front of television. Studies have shown that after five hours, grades begin to go down, along with the desire to read.

Ibid. November 1989, p.25: "Domesticating Your 'Wild' One." ...You may think television is doing you a favor by keeping Danielle the Dervish from whirling, but you're mistaken. TV only prevents kids from learning how to occupy their time creatively. With its constant parade of images, TV will shorten your child's attention span. And the shorter the attention span, the more active the child. If you can't cut out TV completely, limit it to 30 minutes a day.

education, they can gain the functions we have come to consider to be human thinking capacities, including the ability to operate normally during periods of silence.

There are many things that cannot be learned through entertainment. Much of the thought that has come down to us in literature, including the works of classical philosophers, the theologians and ascetic fathers of the Church, not to mention the Bible, is deliberately "incomplete" or "open."[2] The liturgical services of the Church are also in this category, most especially the Divine Liturgy. Like the education offered by a good teacher, everything that is needed is provided. Yet in order to learn, the student is forced to think to draw out the meaning, forced to develop the conclusions on his own, forced to develop his capacity for responding: for responsible and creative thinking. Such books and services, like good teachers, do what no television or visual-aid program can do: they provide a listening atmosphere. They call forth the response that is hidden within. One might say that there is, in effect, a creative mode of silence built into such literature, worship and education. One learns to appreciate this as an opportunity for growth and development. We are not willing to accept the loss of all that is contained within such books and liturgical services, not to mention this creative, educational process. Will our generation perish by destroying the greatest resources of human worth and value along with our planet's natural resources?

The second aspect of this difficulty with silence is that it blocks communication. One cannot truly come to know persons, or the situations and objects around one, without

2 For this insight, I am indebted to remarks in an article by Patrick Mahoney: University of Montreal. "A Psychoanalytic Approach to the Rule of St Benedict." *Monastic Studies* no. 18, Christmas 1988. The Benedictine Priory of Montreal, 1475 Pine Avenue West, Montreal, P.Q., H3G 1B3, Canada.

listening to them and allowing them to reveal themselves. Any knowledge gained without this kind of listening is based more on one's own prejudices than on the reality around us. The research scientist is aware of how crippling such a prejudicial approach can be: the lover of God's creation, including mankind, will take this even more seriously. He will see that this is the greatest underlying cause of the global destruction of our environment.

Yet the person each of us is most responsible for getting to know, the only person for whose life we are ultimately responsible before God, is ourself. We cannot effectively lead others to learn or do what we ourselves have not been able or willing to learn or do. If we are going to learn the best techniques for loving others, we must use only the best techniques for learning to love ourselves. We must begin with the silence that is necessary in order to listen—to ourselves. Self-knowledge has always been looked upon as the "hard and narrow way;" how much more is this true now for those who have been conditioned in many ways from earliest childhood to be unable to cope with silence?

People damaged by parents who would not or could not take the time to listen to them or get to know them as persons, who saw them primarily as terribly annoying interruptions in their lives, find themselves filled with pain and anger. They have learned from their parents that unpleasant things (including themselves) are to be avoided, and their pain and anger give them yet another incentive to flee from silence. One can only rejoice at the great miracle of grace that allows such people at some time in their lives to reach out to others who help them begin to relearn their lessons. The healing of anger and pain begin only when they are faced and acknowledged. A person learns to love and forgive others only when he has learned to love and forgive himself—in silence.

Members of the Church are not exempt from being damaged in this way. Far too often, they have experienced the Christian community of their parish as unable to listen to them any more than their parents or family can. Often, their beginning steps towards healing take them outside the Church to a therapist or "support group." Here at least they find people who listen, and an atmosphere which enables them to respond creatively, perhaps for the first time in their lives. Often their initial reaction will be anger toward the Church for not giving them what these others are offering. They will feel that the Church does not have what such professionals and groups have.

Such a reaction is not surprising and is to be expected. On one level it is absolutely justified. What the Church has to offer is a creative learning and growing experience—it cannot compete as entertainment and be true to itself. Those who get beyond the initial stages of their healing by being listened to in a controlled, therapeutic environment, however, begin to find themselves able to listen in turn. They begin to hear and see things around them that they were too damaged to be aware of before. As they progress in healing, they discover that they are taking only first steps; they are only babes being fed on milk.[3] There is a whole world of adult, Christian maturity that awaits them, into which they can begin to grow for the first time.

It would be a great mistake to turn parishes, seminaries and monasteries into "support groups" or clinics for professional therapy, however. Such bodies within the Church have another purpose: they are to be schools in the best sense. Just as a parish priest or seminary dean or monastic superior does not normally try to do open heart surgery on community members, or set their broken bones, so they ought not to take on these other roles. Having said this, however, there is no

3 Cf. 1 Corinthians 3:2.

doubt that the parishes, seminaries and monasteries, beginning with their leaders, should certainly be aware of where such help can be obtained and give encouragement to those who sense a call to such ministry. It should also be said that they should have the humility to get such help for themselves when they need it, just as they get medical attention for critical problems. Insofar as they themselves have not experienced healing listening in their lives, cannot stand in silent prayer before God, cannot learn from the Scriptures and services of the Church unless they are changed into entertainment events, they cannot themselves be teachers for others. Those who admit their limitations in these regards and begin to get remedial help, especially when they are in positions of leadership, will ultimately be of far greater help to those with them. They will be able to understand the struggles of others "from the bottom up."

Those who reach the point of beginning to listen to themselves in silence find that, paradoxically, they are not alone. In silence, what even non-believers today have come to call their "higher power," reveals Himself as a vital presence. Blessed are those who have the resources of Orthodox teaching to know that this presence is that of their Creator, who loves them to the point of dying for them on the Cross. Knowing that He created us and knows us far better than we know ourselves, and "that He died for us while we were yet sinners,"[4] brings them into the presence of His healing Spirit, which is far more personal, loving, and powerful than any of the created, finite persons who may have mis-loved them in the past. He acts to heal what none of us can do or heal for ourselves or for others, even though we do begin to mediate His healing love and presence to and for one another as we come to participate in Him.

4   Romans 5:8.

Let us who call ourselves Christians and perhaps even teachers of others begin to enter into this fellowship of our God. In silence and prayer, let us come to know Him, ourselves, one another, and the whole of creation, as we exist together in the Trinity of Persons who creates, sustains and redeems all things and all men.

4

Gifts

"What do you have that you did not receive? And if you received it, why do you boast as if it were not a gift?"[1]

Should we write one more sermon on keeping the Spirit of Christ in Christmas? On getting past the commercialization of the feast by using pious gifts, gimmicks and slogans to counteract those of Madison Avenue bombarding us from every side the minute summer shows any signs of cooling down? On giving twice by buying from the (religious) charity of your choice?

Let us rather side-step all of that here. "To the pure, all things are pure."[2] It is still possible to rejoice in the feast; in the giving and receiving of gifts as well as in the traditional church services, family gatherings and customs; even in the spirit of happy celebration that manages to catch up with the irreligious who are swept along the aisles of twinkling lights and teddy bears in discount department stores. We hope every one of you experiences at least one moment of pure joy over the birth of true Life into this world.

Sadly, many will not. "To the corrupt and unbelieving nothing is pure."[3] We would like to be able to say that we are in the camp of pure and holy Orthodox Christians, who can discern what is good and true, keeping ourselves free from wrinkle, stain and spot in the world. We want to be that. At

1 1 Corinthians 4:7.
2 Titus 1:15.
3 Ibid.

times, we can even see what is good and true in spite of ourselves; we manage that. Or rather, for whole minutes, letting
go of our own fallen ideas, words and behavior, we receive the
grace to let God live and act through us.

Far too often, however, our lives are simply one more sad
commentary on the late twentieth century. If we do not use
cocaine, alcohol, food, sex, television or cigarettes in an
abusive or addictive way, we have still probably managed to
come up with our own tricks that allow us to escape from the
unpleasant realities of our daily life and the relationships and
situations around us.

Within reason, of course, distancing ourselves from pain
can be healthy. One part of the gift of life God has given us is
the ability temporarily to block out emotional and physical
pain. What He had in mind for this part of His gift and what we
do with it, of course, may be two very different things. Rather
than using pleasure and work to re-create us, to return us,
refreshed and renewed, to acceptance of our life—we often try
to substitute them for life and reality. What is meant to be on
occasion healthy and holy recreation is frequently used instead
for permanent escape.

Why? What causes our generation to be so vulnerable to
avoiding the realities of life? Historians, sociologists and others
continuously analyze the sweeping trends that characterize
North American culture and society and that are moving across
the globe as surely as atmospheric pollution and acid rain. But
what about just me? I received my introduction to all of this
through very particular channels: my parents, my extended
family, my friends, the churches and schools I attended, the
books I read, the television I watched... Perhaps it is not too late
to renounce all of these, to become my own person.

Yet all of these were also the channels for every gift of
good that came from God: my very life, my ability to love,

think, speak, write, create... If I think I can remove all evil, guilt and sin from my life by cutting off everything I have ever known, I have to face the possibility that I may also be cutting off all that is good, true, pure and holy. So at least on some levels, this is more than a simple problem with an equally simple solution.

What if I turn to meditation and prayer? That sounds good. In fact, there is no other way, but if I try taking a few steps along this way, without at least as much basic preparation as a scout would make before setting out on a survival weekend in a state park, I will probably get nowhere except into trouble. That is, if I am serious about becoming what God made and gifted me to be.

The trouble I may easily be in before I even start along the way is believing that any meditation or prayer will do. Yet many people are able to use periods of quiet, repeated words for clearing the mind, inspiring reading and thoughts, for ends that have nothing whatever to do with the God who created and redeemed us. They may discover that they can hold their temper more easily and so become more popular or successful, even in business and at parties, through these methods. Or they may find that they gain a sense of distance from the crowd, together with a feeling of peaceful superiority, even in church.

For myself, I have learned that I have to be sure I know where I am headed before I even start along this way. I have to try to achieve the greatest honesty I can muster at any given time. I have to face my own unbelief and ask: "God"—perhaps even: "if there is a God,"—"reveal Yourself to me as You are and not just as I believe You to be." If I do this, I will eventually have to accept that I am coming into the presence of a Person far more alive, powerful and real than I am. I will begin to see that He insists on being Himself the way, and that often He has very little to do with my own ideas about paths and "inner journeys." He will gradually let me see that the obstacles along the path are within myself. I can no longer blame global trends, or my parents, or the school I attended, or the wealth or poverty I have experienced. He can use anything and everything in creation as the means for bringing me further along this path, even horrible experiences that I and others (including the devil) thought were the final, destructive word. He will let silence become a way in which I learn to listen and He is able to speak. He will allow books to come my way with passages that suddenly cause things to make sense where before there was only confusion. People I have known for years may suddenly say or do some very familiar thing, and I will be given the grace to hear or see the meaning for the first time. Periods of trouble or crisis around me which rob me of my times of silence, the words of my prayer books, or familiar loved ones, become the push I need to get up from a comfortable resting place to move further along the way.

Gradually, as He sees that I am getting used to the idea, He even begins to let me see how little honesty I have had. As I continue always to ask Him to reveal Himself to me, I will discover that He also is revealing me to myself as I really am, and not as I have believed myself to be. I will discover that some things I had thought were good about me are in fact very artificial substitutes for the real thing. Other aspects of myself that I preferred to ignore may turn out to be crucial in my life. I will come to see that my passions and instincts, my physical strengths and needs, my mind and emotions, were meant to be brought into godly use, and that I have chosen either to reject them or abuse them. If I have decided that anger, for example, is not a good thing, I may have convinced myself that I do not have any. Because I have not been willing to use it in any healthy and holy way, I will discover that it has burst forth by itself in unhealthy and destructive ways. I may discover that what I considered to be my wit was very thinly screened sarcastic anger. I may pity myself for bouts of depression, only to learn that they are temper tantrums turned inside out. However, once I have been convinced that I have anger and that I need to use it, I will probably instead abuse it for a long time, wallowing in it, justifying its misuse, letting others be the target for it. I will find that saying all the prayers in the world, spending every hour in silence, participating in every church service, will not move me an inch along the way until I have grappled with this anger and learned to use it the way God expects it to be used. It should never be used against people, including myself, but only against evil: the devil, sin and abuse, primarily within myself where they manage to cripple even my right use of anger!

I will have discovered that this way of prayer and meditation comes to include my whole life and also transform my whole life. As I go further I will always discover more in life that is from God and cannot be left out. What I had once seen as the end of my life will turn out to be a door along the way, opening directly into Christ. But before I may open that door, coming to see that as He is and as I am, I can love and be no other, I must use every possible day, hour and minute to gather up the whole of my life so that I may eternally walk in God.

5

Purity of Heart

Friends have written to us about the struggle not to have a divided heart in the world. At times, it seems almost impossible to have anything else. How can we live as pilgrims, with our hearts in the heavenly city that is our true home? There is so much in today's world that reaches out and grabs our attention, even when we want to be looking elsewhere: homes with family problems and social and financial pressures, not to mention such things as hard rock and television; jobs—or the loss of jobs—that force us to deal with people and situations we would otherwise avoid; stores that assault our every sense in their attempt to sell us a way of life that makes their merchandise a necessity for us...

In the world the Lord leads each of us Christians in a different way. Ultimately, however, we all need to grow into a realization that if we are to keep our sanity, He is the only one who can have undivided mastery over our heart. We will discover that this also means making room for all the others He puts into our lives. It isn't a matter of dividing our love—it is learning to multiply it.

We have to be watchful when relationships or interests seem to upset the balance and seem to push the Lord out. Yet eventually, if we are honest, we see that this can be only an appearance: it is an aspect of the Lord's great humility and seeming weakness in the face of the human propensity to worship idols. The other people and things we may idolize would not be present to us if He had not allowed them to be. Gradually we can come to see Him through them as well as loving Him as His own Person in Christ. He is not just one among our many (or few) close loved ones, interests and friends—He is the foundation, framework, atmosphere and goal of all our loves.

So often not understanding that the Lord is the center of all life causes heartbreak in marriages and friendships, not to mention monastic vocations. A career, another person, even a whole community, cannot be God, and eventually the longings, desires and needs we have that God alone can fulfill place a "burden too hard to be borne" on others. And we in turn begin to feel cheated and resentful. God is merciful, and He lets us try to manage with just our work, our friends or spouse, until we are ready to face the abyss of our need and desire: our need for God our Savior.

Is there some way to test whether we should try to strive for such purity of heart in a particular situation or relationship? Is the life of a single person dedicated to a worthwhile career or service the right way? Or marriage? Or the monastic life? Friends ask us this, also. We will limit ourselves to discussing the monastic life, since it is what we know from experience. Yet it seems to us that for those who are seeking God in this way, and not looking upon the Church as just one more activity to be scheduled around the rest of their lives, the same basic principles will apply wherever God may lead them.

In theory, there should not be any one type of person, or even a special cluster of attributes, appropriate for the monastic life. Given the realities of the American Church and the very tiny sprouts of communities that exist, however, some things which could be absorbed by larger communities become overwhelming in close quarters. And in each community in particular, there are other challenges, based on the circumstances, work and daily life that are possible there.

Basic physical, mental and emotional health, a desire for the Church and its life of service and sacraments, proven ability to be responsible and willing to work, plus the inner resources to function even when there is not a great deal of external excitement or stimulation are normally necessities.

But any true Christian vocation is a matter of faith. All of the human abilities we have just described cannot take the place of a live and growing relationship with the Lord, sustained daily by personal prayer, and a firm sense that He is the one who makes the decisions in our lives and gives what is necessary to fulfill them. The monastic life purposely leaves very little room to avoid such striving toward purity of heart.

If the desire to seek God is present, and going to a specific community seems to be the door He has opened, then He will provide what is necessary. This is the case even when (not if) such people find themselves obviously out of their depth, humanly speaking, in the midst of situations where they discover that they can learn to be humble only when they can accept being humiliated, and learn to place their trust completely in God only by having their own powers disclosed as the limited human things they are.

A basic sense of God-given worth is also necessary—humility is not meant to take that away. In the world, material and financial assets can be obvious symbols of what a person has been able to achieve. For a person who goes on to monastic life, such a step should not destroy that sense of achievement. It should provide an opportunity to attempt to work on realizing the spiritual reality that underlies the symbol. We will all have to come to this realization after death on Judgment Day. We need to be able to continue to see ourselves as children of God with the great worth and beauty He created us to have even when the external signs are not there. The monastic life is an attempt to "take the bull by the horns," as the saying goes, and test ourselves in this regard while we are still in a position on this earth to do something about it.

This is the reason why the martyrs are so much a part of the monastic daily services. They focus most clearly our desire to be able to witness to all that is good, true, pure and holy; all that the Lord has done for us, even when it seems that circumstances and other people are trying to take everything, even our life, away. We are not meant deliberately to humiliate, deprive and hurt each other in order to achieve this. We can be sure that the humiliations, deprivations and hurts will come. The great strength of Christian friends is the ability to support one another in going through such things in a growing spirit of personal repentance, not blaming others, giving in to despair or self-pity, or avoiding the Cross.

In such a spirit, we can persevere through whatever comes with joy, even when that joy is not on the level of ecstatic delight. Such joy is a matter of spiritual strength, coming from only one source: the belief that God does provide.

Those who try to live this life would claim that it is not hopeless idealism, but true, hard-nosed reality. For every Christian, life is a continuing struggle for purity of heart. However we pursue it, our final goal is God and the life that only He can give in the Kingdom beyond all struggle and death, where He has gone by His own Passion and Resurrection. May we be worthy to enter into this Kingdom, tasting it even now in the moments of feast and celebration we share in the Church. Let us greet one another: Christ is Risen! Indeed He is Risen!

6

Maturity

What is maturity? Is it what most of us look forward to from the time we are quite small: the day when, having reached what appears to us to be maturity, we will be beyond having to change and grow, and can rest on our laurels, basking in the rosy glow of accomplishment? From the day of our conception we have suffered from youth and its painful ignorance; from the mistakes made by immature judgment. How we long to be beyond these stages, filled with wisdom, taking our place among the ranks of mature men and women!

We, however, believe that maturity for men and women is the disciplined state reached when they finally realize that here we are only beginning a process that continues forever, leading us from glory to glory, growing eternally into the unending fullness of God. Immaturity is not such growth; rather, immaturity is the refusal to grow beyond a certain point of normal development. Immaturity does not look ahead to what is to come and to those who go before as guides but clings to the familiar past in fear. Immaturity refuses to be taught, to be "discipled;" it has for its standard only its own past thoughts and behavior.

We have all known children whom we would call mature, not because they look and act like miniature adults, but because they are fully at their level of development, not holding on to behavior that was appropriate for them earlier but which they have now outgrown. We have known adults, ourselves included, who seemed to have reached a certain state of maturity, but under stress, pressure or adversity have reverted to words and behavior that can only be called childish and self-centered. We have also met mature adults whose presence we were led to honor, yet who had a childlike quality of joy, freedom, trust and love as they looked upon others and the world.

We would also say that none of us on Judgment Day will be able to use the times, people and surroundings where God in His providence has placed us as excuses for not growing fully into what He intends. We are given a share in the Spirit that lives beyond time and place, that gives us the discernment to know what is right and what is wrong no matter what is being done around us.[1] While it is true that we can and do learn from one another and even normally should, true knowledge comes from God.[2] Those who truly seek, find.[3] The analogy of electricity is often used to describe the work of the Holy Spirit. When the normal, God-given channels of the Church are working, we receive knowledge, grace and truth in traditional ways. This comes through books, events and the words of others and of the Church, much as the electrical wiring of a house quietly provides us with heat and light. Yet when these God-given channels are missing either through lack of opportunity or the sinfulness of man, then the Spirit will break through like a bolt of lightning if need be, cutting across the preconceived ideas and arrangements of men.[4]

For Orthodox Christians, Jesus Christ Himself, given to us through the teaching, tradition, scripture and sacraments of the Church, is the primary source for our understanding of human maturity. Today, even in the fallen human society which surrounds us, very few people would argue that Jesus was not an historical person. There are many who regard Him as only a teacher, yet even they frequently acknowledge that He was one of the greatest teachers, a brilliant intellect, a charismatic personality with an intuitive and penetrating mind. As we know

1   See for example 1 John 2, especially verses 20, 21 and 27.
2   Matthew 16:17, Galatians 1:11-12ff.
3   Matthew 7:7.
4   Acts 2:1-36, 9:1-22, 10:44-11:18.

from the Gospel accounts of his demanding ministry, he was a person of powerful physique and stature. It is important for us to remember that He was all those things. He was a real human being, so that very few people who met Him were able to make the leap to a recognition that He was the Son of God and God.

Yet those who have not been given the gift to see sometimes believe that when He made statements about being equal to God he was under the mild delusion of a misguided egomaniac. We in the Church, on the other hand, see Him making these statements as the first witness to the truth, the first martyr. His life and death are not for us just a tale of human promise ending in failure and tragedy, but rather the story of Truth in Person entering into the worst of human life. His truthfulness as well as His suffering and death have been vindicated through the ultimate triumph of the Resurrection.

In the Gospel record, as much as Jesus included children in His ministry and used children as examples to his own disciples,[5] it seems that His main ministry was as an adult to adults. He Himself grew as normal children grew, "increasing in wisdom and in stature."[6] When Luke gives us a vignette of His being in the temple at the age of twelve, even though "all who heard him were amazed at his understanding and his answers,"[7] he also makes clear that Jesus was not there as a teacher, but as a learner: "They found Him in the temple, sitting among the teachers, listening to them and asking them questions."[8]

"Jesus, when He began His ministry, was about thirty years of age..."[9] In spite of His obvious maturity as a child, the incarnate God waited to begin His ministry. He already had the

5 For example, Mark 9:36, Matthew 18:3.
6 Luke 2:52.
7 Luke 2:47.
8 Luke 2:46
9 Luke 3:23.

skills and maturity to be known as a carpenter,[10] but He did not try to be something more before it was the right time, any more than He held onto his youthful work and behavior when they were no longer appropriate. He neither avoided nor grasped at anything, neither equality to God, nor job security and social status, nor His human reputation as the Jewish Messiah, nor even life itself. He went through all the stages of His life when the time had come for each, and it is our belief that He continues to do so, bringing each of us into the eternal life of God which we share with Him in our saved humanity.

In the Body of Christ which is the Church, it seems that God can act without the proper structures when fallen human beings have not allowed them to be in place or have "short-circuited" them through sin. It seems also that He sees these structures as temporary expedients put in place for our own growth into maturity: "And His gifts were that some should be apostles, some prophets, some evangelists, some pastors and teachers, for the equipping of the saints, for the work of ministry, for building up the body of Christ, *until* we all attain to the unity of the faith and of the knowledge of the Son of God, to mature manhood, to the measure of the stature of the fullness of Christ; so that we may no longer be children, tossed to and fro and carried about with every wind of doctrine, by the cunning of men, by their craftiness in deceitful wiles. Rather, speaking the truth in love, we are to grow up in every way into him who is the head, into Christ..."[11]

"And no longer shall each man teach his neighbor and each his brother, saying, 'Know the Lord,' for they shall all know me, from the least of them to the greatest, says the Lord"[12]

"And I saw no temple in the city, for its temple is the Lord God the Almighty and the Lamb."[13]

10 Mark 6:3.
11 Ephesians 4:11-15.
12 Jeremiah 31:34.

Thus, even the structures of the Church as we know them should not become ends in themselves, but the means by which we grow into ever increasing maturity and dependence on God alone. We need crutches in our weakness and infirmity, and let us not try to do without them before it is time, or we will never grow strong in love and obedience for Christ. But when the divine Physician sets us free, let us be ready to run the race with boldness.

This vision of maturity can be understood only within the vision of the divine humanity we share in Christ. Outside the Church, the rigid external observances of the scribes and pharisees will always give an appearance of adult behavior. For those within the Church, hearing the Scriptural accounts of how vigorously the Lord worked to embarrass such behavior and how hard St Paul and others fought in the early Church to replace it with the freedom and discernment of God's Holy Spirit, there will always be something more: eternally there will be all the fullness of God.

13 Revelation 21:22.

7

The Monastic Life Today

Those desiring to embark on the monastic vocation must understand from the beginning that they are by definition aiming for a solitary vocation. The word monastic, from the Greek *monachos,* means "one who is alone." This is the conclusion that comes from reading the monastic fathers—even those most supportive of community life. Hermit, in its root sense deriving from *eremitike,* meaning "one who dwells in the desert or wilderness," is another universal monastic definition.

Sometimes, as in Russia, even large monasteries such as Optina and Sarov were called "deserts" (*pustyni*). Indeed, community life comes as a by-product of one's turning from what one has relied upon for support in order to go into the wilderness to place oneself entirely in God's hands.

Christian solitary life reflects the Lord's own experience, which in turn sums up the experience of Israel, of being driven by the Spirit into the wilderness for a full period ("40 days" or "40 years") of prayer and fasting in order to confront the devil and his temptations and to show them for what they are before the face of God. It is fulfilled in a lifetime of repentance, growth and development. Alone in the wilderness, a person comes, through prayer, to have an ever-growing experience of God's love and redeeming work. There, the prayerful attempt to enter into the moral and ascetic life of the Church, including its personal channels of obedience, leads to a growing sense of one's own sinful betrayal of that love and work. Thus one comes through repentance to a growing openness to them. One's relationships with others come to be based more on the freedom of

God's love and far less on one's own merely human needs or such needs in the community. One's spiritual senses become sharpened to know the communion we have with God and with one another even when the presence of God and of others is not apprehended by the exterior senses. One radically rejects any lesser agendas, with all "earthly cares," in order to have one's life entirely transformed, filled and led by God. For some, like St Seraphim and our own Father Herman, this means that the Lord in his providence returns them from a life of solitude in the wilderness periodically or permanently in order to be an immediate revelation of God and the Kingdom to others. Some, on the other hand, always remain hidden in God. As Zossima said to Mary of Egypt, it was through her prayers during those long years in the Egyptian desert when no one knew anything about her that God was preserving the church and the world.

This is the spiritual reverse of Dostoevsky's saying that the least impure thought a person harbors in the most hidden recesses of his soul pollutes the universe. A person who places himself so radically in the wilderness climate of prayer and allows himself to be transformed by God can have a healing effect on the entire universe. Such a person becomes a "co-savior" of the universe as he participates in and focuses Christ's work of salvation in his time. This will have an effect on the material universe, since the material universe expresses spiritual realities. Still, the monastic is one who should be the last to forget that "our struggle is not against flesh and blood, but against the principalities, against the powers, against the world rulers of this present darkness, against the spiritual hosts of wickedness in the heavenly places."[1]

There is a Hasidic saying that God keeps the world going because of the prayers of a small number of hidden "pious ones." Christians also have this faith. If not a single hidden, pi-

1   Ephesians 6:12.

ous one can be found on the earth, one whose work is concentrated solely on spiritual warfare, the powers of darkness will have their day. We are perilously close to this in our time.

Universal, spiritual community, our unity in the Body of Christ, is the natural home of redeemed mankind—and other communities on earth reflect this to a greater or lesser degree. A human community in and of itself, however, may be only a distorted reflection of the presence of the "divine community" of the Holy Trinity. Such a merely human community will not bring healing.

Men and women often come to monasteries today "seeking community." They are rarely satisfied or healed because they have not come seeking God who alone can satisfy and heal them. The "one thing needful" that could transform and renew their being and life is rejected in the name of "community." Such an idolatrous view of community is common today. "Community" becomes an end in itself, and as such it is not found. The desert experience, to be alone with God for the sake of being united with all in him, is the last thing that some people want, even in a monastery.

In God's providence, therapeutic support groups and tools for psychological and emotional healing are available to us in ways that they were not before. They have never been so needed, and the Church will need to use all of them. Support groups are as close as many people can get to true community, given where they are coming from, and they are absolutely necessary for people at certain times in their lives. Like all the stages of development, however, they must be transcended when they have served their purpose. If they are clung to for too long, they become unhealthy for their participants.

It is rare today for a person to come from a family or parish that has offered support adequate for spiritual growth. Most aspirants to monastic life need time in specific, therapeutic situations, followed by time in some form of pre-monastic spiritual community, before they can begin to comprehend monastic or eremetic life and the type of community that comes and grows with this specific calling.

Some people, however, have come through our dehumanizing society with the ability to respond with a degree of faithfulness to God's call to a monastic life. They have come to see the need for the Church and for personal repentance for their own sins, the sins of others and the sins of the world. They should not lose heart because they see they are so far from participating in God's love and perfection. They must rather be "faithful in little" here in this life, so that they may be accounted worthy of the fullness of life in God's Kingdom.[2]

Those called to the monastic way must go into the ascetic wilderness as St Herman did, not to tame it, but to accept it on its own terms and allow it to teach them its own unique lessons, including how to handle hardship and deprivation in total dependence on God, as it has taught a multitude of Orthodox monastics for centuries. They must allow themselves to be weaned from merely natural supports as far as God desires and permits through the providence of their capabilities and circumstances, so that they can live entirely for God and solely by his will. This is the whole point of their life.

Monastics cannot ask to see in the Church what they are not struggling for in their own lives. On one level, they need the example or help of others in order to learn how to place God at the center and to cast down the various idols that tempt them from His true worship. On another level, they will come to realize that when they do not find inspiration, understanding and support in those around them, this lack is allowed by God for their growth and testing. In all situations, the monastic must live for God alone.

2 Luke 16:10.

8

The Monastery, the Parish and the Church

From our reading of the history of the Church and the development of monasticism within it, we know that from the first, "monasticism" (a term meaning life lived alone,) was simply one of the lifestyles found within the parish. Often this monasticism was not very organized: a single widow might be "set apart" to live the rest of her life in prayer, in a state of consecrated celibacy, without personal possessions. She would be provided for by the parish and live under the guidance of the local bishop. Or a small group of deaconesses, set apart by the bishop to minister to the needs of the women, would also accept a life of celibacy. Following the example of the first "parish" in Jerusalem, they would hold all things in common, coming together for regular worship and meals. We know that even before St Anthony the Great founded monasticism for men, virgins lived together for both spiritual and material support.

In those early days, the Church, in her parishes, rapidly developed a way of life that allowed her to survive through the centuries in an immoral, pluralistic society. She also survived the persecution that society inflicted on those whose moral and spiritual standards challenged its own. In such surroundings, Christians—parish members—knew they greatly needed to support one another in the high calling of the Faith. They knew they could not attempt to live lives of prayer and holiness, with the discipline and moral fiber that requires, if they did not spend time together. They needed time for learning and sharing what was known from the past and what they came to know from experience. They also needed time for shared worship and thanksgiving, for offering God the service of praise as members of the Royal Priesthood. They knew that however they might live in the world, they could not be "of the world" and follow their Master. They certainly were not able to stamp out sin, or remove the temptation to "go native," but these temptations were seen for what they were, and the truly faithful struggled to gain something greater.

That immoral, pluralistic society was finally brought to its knees before such groups of Christians—the parishes of the early fourth century. There is no question that a great victory was won, yet as is the case with most victories on this earth, the vanquished end up conquering the conqueror. Perhaps only in these last times do we see the full consequences. We see a Church that still seems to believe she can live on easy terms with society, so that she often seems not to see that society's standards for both personal and corporate conduct have become as opposed to her own as they were during the first three Christian centuries.

The response of many Christians to the victory of the Church in the fourth century was a healthy one. They saw the necessity of stretching the tightly-knit family organization of parishes to let in those who, because of their large numbers and their ignorance, could not immediately adopt the whole Christian life, which required one to show love through prayer, morality and personal discipline. Even the Apostles often failed to lead people into such a life: St Paul had alarmed a Roman governor who seemed interested in the Faith until he heard about "justice and self control and future judgment."[1] A rich young man walked away from the Lord Himself when He suggested, "If you want to be perfect, go and sell all your possessions and give them to the poor and come, follow me."[2]

1   Acts 24:25.
2   Matthew 19:21.

Many recognized a calling within themselves no less important and demanding than teaching and laboring among the hordes of new converts, a vocation to grow in their own Christian lives. Armed with love and discipline, they were called to fight "not against flesh and blood, but against the principalities, against the powers, against the world rulers of this present darkness, against the spiritual hosts of wickedness in the heavenly places."[3] Men and women withdrew alone or gathered in groups to support one another in this spiritual warfare. The great monastic age of the Church had begun, which has lasted down to our present century.

It seems that in the early days, these "monastics" were still considered part of the closest parish, although they had their own daily cycle of the prayer and liturgical services following a pattern that the earliest Church had inherited from its Jewish roots. They were lay men and women, and would participate in the Eucharist at times when a priest from the parish was free to come to them. When priests came to be accepted into men's communities, their separation from the parish became greater. As women's communities desired a more regular sacramental life, the bishop also appointed priests to serve them. So what may appear to be a specialized form of parish evolved, with its own priest and unique congregation, just as seminaries developed to train leaders for the Church and also took on the appearance of a specialized form of parish. Perhaps in our time of changing forms, these appearances will also change. We pray that God will guide us in this. We do not need change for the sake of change—we do need to be able to see that wherever we Christians find ourselves, we are members one of another. Our parishes, monasteries, seminaries and other groups together reveal to the world the Body of Christ on earth.

3 Ephesians 6:12.

9

Family Life and the Monastery

Men and women living in a monastery are often called a family. Even the terms we use for one another: Mother, Father Sister, Brother, are family terms. Most parish and "home" families today have had little opportunity to meet monks and nuns, to ask them about their life and share in the services and the quiet, prayerful atmosphere of the monastery. We are often amazed at the "notions" people have about us! No, we are not born in our habits. Yes, we must work to support ourselves as any family does—we must buy food, heat our houses in winter, pay our insurance bills, and if we are a women's monastery, pay our priest a salary. No, we do not get any regular stipend from the Church for this. The monastery is not an escape for us. A man or woman who is incapable of normal family life and who cannot hold a job will find the life of a monastic family even more demanding! We do not have T.V., we do not "go out" socially. In fact, we do not have many of the "escapes" most people use today without even realizing they are doing so.

We came to the monastery because we believe this is where God has called us. We believe He has given us enough love and security in our own lives that we want to go further; we want to learn to love even when it is not easy. We do not come to the monastery because our family has failed us, or because we have had a "bad experience"—although no doubt we have had our share of them. We come because we want to spend our lives specializing in love, growing to be the men and women God created us to be. If we are prepared to take on the disciplines of the monastic life, it is most likely that we did experience love growing up in our own families. Now we want to be true brothers and sisters in Christ to all—not just to those for whom we feel a natural affinity or (in our culture) a sexual attraction. We know such love is possible: Christ and many of His saints have shown us this love.

We are not likely these days to just "drift" into a monastery "by accident." We have grown up and lived with the same pressures from our society and even in our church that make stable Christian marriages rare today. We also were conditioned by advertisements, television, politicians, schools and the atmosphere of drugs, sex, gurus and cults that surrounds us all. We did not realize this until we tried to grow in a different direction. Indeed it may seem to people that a person who believes he or she is called to the monastic way of life must be "different," if not downright strange. How can we believe that God has called us in our days without at least the sort of blinding revelation St Paul received on the road to Damascus? Perhaps we did have such a call, or our experience of life was interrupted by an event that made us think beyond the usual terms.

How much better it is, however, when children grow up in parishes and families where learning to pray, to listen to God, becomes a normal part of daily life. It is a great blessing when people realize that they need the Church—even all those repetitious phrases and litanies in church services—in order to break the spell that television advertising especially has cast over us. It has led us to lead lives that are more animal than truly human. When men and women place themselves in the presence of what they know to be true, pure, holy and beautiful, they begin to reflect that truth, purity, holiness and beauty in their daily lives. They see that wherever we are, God has given us, through the Church, the atmosphere we need to live in; He has given us the Holy Spirit to teach us that we are never alone, never forced to "sell out" what we know to be right and true. They say that the Church is truly our family and furthermore is not just one of the activities of our busy week to be fitted in around our "real life." Parishes and families that begin to live this way discover their humanity.

This is the type of human family we try to be in our monastic community. We know we cannot live such a family life in isolation. May we all be guided and strengthened by the Lord to become the families we need to be if we are to grow into the full stature of the maturity of Christ.

10

The Call to a Monastic Way of Christian Living

"The health and maturity of the Church are indicated by the state of its monastic life." This is a statement often heard among American Orthodox. And indeed, even though monastic communities in this country are small and relatively new, we find that financial and other material support is given very generously, and even sacrificially, by many people. Sometimes, however, we discover that people may be puzzled when we do what has always been done everywhere down the ages by monastics who have tried to live their life seriously.

A monastery is a place where a woman goes because she believes she is meant to grow in her relationship with God through prayer, and she wants Him and that prayer above everyone and everything else. For such a woman, giving up the pursuit of marriage, good times, fun, an attractive appearance, a career etc., is not a "sacrifice" in the pejorative way that word is so often used. It is the means she herself greatly desires because of the goal she sees before her. A tragedy of our times is that there are very few places left where a woman can find these means.

If a woman sees the monastic life as a "terrible sacrifice," this is normally a sign that God is not calling her to it. The life of a Christian in the world is the way of testing what God has worked out for many; and for them, lives of holiness that please God will continue to grow in our churches. For those of us who do want the monastic life, however, who see why silence and long hours of liturgical prayer—along with all the other very definite disciplines of the monastic life—are what we need, it is the path we take to grow as God intends us to do.

There are times when following this way can be hard, and it is certainly not "fun and games," but for those who are called it is a far safer road than any we could mark out for ourselves. We look to Christ, and try to "walk as He walked."[1] There are times when the life of any disciple of Christ may be like the Garden of Gethsemane and Golgotha, and he may be called to suffer as He suffered. But when this is a true Cross, taken up in the spirit of Christ, there will be joy in the suffering, just as the Lord did not look upon His "going up to Jerusalem"[2] as a "horrible sacrifice" He was "forced to make." He did it freely and "for the joy that was set before Him."[3]

Many of those who begin seeking the monastic way read the Gospel and hear the Lord's words to "leave all and follow me."[4] They may read the lives of the saints—for example, the life of St Seraphim of Sarov, the greatly beloved Nineteenth Century saint of Russia—and come to realize that he was not just an odd person who could not do anything else with his life but stand alone on a rock and pray. They may have understood that through him God has given a lesson they need to learn well: "Save your own soul first; then a thousand around you will be saved." The days and nights St Seraphim spent standing alone in terrible conditions were the God-given means that brought him freedom from his fallen ego and participation in the life of God. "Save your own soul; then a thousand around you will be saved." We come for that. We come seeing that our own life is in great need of God's healing and salvation. In "saving one's own soul," we learn with St Paul that "it is God who works

1 Cf. 1 John 2:6.
2 Luke 9:51.
3 Hebrews 12:2.
4 Mark 10:28-31.

within us to save."[5] He can use us, if this life of prayer is His will for us, to work in those thousand others far more effectively than we ever could by our own efforts.

We do need strong support in this way, however. The Lord himself rebuked Simon Peter ("Get behind me, Satan!") when Peter suggested that He ought not to have to suffer.[6] He needed understanding from His disciples to do what He came to do, not false comfort and sympathy. A real trial for nuns is the person who offers them some "treat" that they have very deliberately given up, knowing it is not in their own best interest.

Yet, please God, even though we strive to give up much of what the world seems to offer us, we will live, daily mindful of where we are. We live in a world and a Church filled with people in great need of love, in a Church that needs to accomplish its mission to equip its own people as ministers to the rest of God's creation. Missionary endeavors seem sometimes to be attempts to bring the gospel of material comfort to those in foreign countries with a lower standard of living. Seeking to give up much of that material comfort ourselves leads us to question whether a different work of mission is not needed in our own country. Even without television and the aid of the daily news, we cannot help but see a growing poverty here. It is far more destructive, though non-material. We see men and women who substituting power struggles for love and communication with each other even in the Church, prosperous adults who can live only by using alcohol and other mind-altering substances, teenagers whose response to what they have been given is suicide. We see "cradle Orthodox" who enter a denomination or cult in order to have an experience of spiritual life that is the Church's own

5 Philippians 2:13.
6 Matthew 16:23.

legacy, infants sold to the pornography industry or worse, not to mention the very material consequences of our "western life-style," the growing numbers of homeless people in the United States who are no longer only the lazy and dysfunctional. These are the thousands around us we know the Lord wills to save.

If being sane means living the same life as the world, then we certainly are not sane. When rough times come, like the present, when prices are soaring and new tax laws are leading people to cut support drastically for all non-profit and charitable organizations, we may even wonder if we can continue to follow the healing discipline of the monastic life to which God has called us. Yet we know we need it in our own lives far more than St Seraphim needed it in his. We know that for any Christian the answer is not to abandon what God calls them to do. We struggle to cease being "functional atheists." We struggle not only to believe in God with our minds, but also to accept in our daily lives that He is in control of everything, even our own sins and the hard times around us and in the Church. None of us in today's world can see the future, but we can trust that whatever it holds is meant for our salvation.

11

Challenged by Freedom

Often a monk or nun is asked: "Why did you enter the monastery?" Answers to this question are as many and varied as the people who give them. God's calling of each person is as unique as he or she is, both in history and in the eternal life of God's Kingdom.

There are some common threads running through all the answers, though, and we would like to write about one of them, though we are aware that this can be a partial answer at best. Only Jesus Himself was able to approach His vocation with total purity of heart. The rest of us make do with the best we can manage at the time. As more than one experienced monastic has put it: "I came for all the wrong reasons, but God used the opportunity to show me the right ones, and I have stayed because of them."

This particular reason first shows itself as a challenge. People meet or hear about the monastic life, and it is entirely different from anything they have known in their experience. They often have a very negative reaction to learning about the way monks and nuns live. The life appears to be inhuman, unlivable for a normal person. Celibacy appears to be a perversion; a lifetime of repentance and obedience, sheer masochism.

For most people the understanding of the monastic life goes no further. But others go on to meet or hear about a particular monk or nun, and their presuppositions are destroyed. Rather than being perverted, the person they meet is very healthy and "together," with a sense of joy—even a sense of humor. This is not a spineless person, incapable of thinking in-

dependently or making decisions. Rather, they find themselves in the presence of a strong personality with definite beliefs and a sense of responsibility for his or her own life. Moreover, the person they meet seems to know and understand
them and to accept them as they are.

Mulling over this new experience, such people find
themselves revising their thoughts and opinions. From what
they know about the disciplines this monastic practices, he or
she ought not to be normal. Something does not fit.

Struggling with this thought can suggest something that
looks a bit like climbing Mount Everest or becoming a
gold-medal athlete at the Olympics. Obviously, more than the
usual human resources are required in each of these circumstances. Yet the monastic challenge may appear even greater
because it involves the daily, physical discipline of the ascetic
life with no complete vacations: self control in food, sleep,
sex, and so on that every person in rigorous training under-
takes. In addition it means growing in love and grace through
the practices. A monastic cannot be excused for being an awful
person the way a star athlete often is by our society.

While almost anyone can appear to be joyful, contented
and loving when things are going their way, the monastic
seeks the freedom to be joyful, contented and loving even
when things are terrible. He does not seek to grow in
self-denial in order to become an automaton. He seeks rather
to free himself from the slavery that prevents him from being
the mature person that he sees he can be in Christ. He will begin by avoiding the obvious addictions such as drugs and alcohol, but he will come to see that this is just a beginning. As he
grows in discernment, he begins to see new struggles with
what he can only call the demons that possess him.

Only God living within us gives us our total freedom.
Addiction, possession, magic, all leave us at best passive, at

worst, crippled or dead. In his preface to his translation of *The Ladder of Divine Ascent* by St John Climacus, Colm Liubheid writes about "the undeniable correlation between hardship and an intense marshalling of inner, and frequently unsuspected, resources."[1] This can be true, but only for those who are able to accept such hardship voluntarily. For every saint that has come out of a prison or concentration camp, hundreds more have come out bitter and twisted, resenting the torture and the life and comforts they feel were stolen from them. It is not coincidence that monks and nuns and others of deep religious faith are the ones who are able to grow and find freedom even in the midst of the worst tortures and hardships.

Yet an Orthodox monastery is not meant to be a prison or concentration camp. It is, on the contrary, a very sensitive training school. In addition to providing a full sacramental life, a monastery has as powerful teaching tools the liturgical services, instruction and sharing by those who are experienced, and readings in Scripture and other good books. This is all necessary to enable the obedience of rational creatures, not irrational beasts. There is also training in the work of the monastery, beginning with the normal obedience of apprenticeship.

No one may force a person to enter and undertake particular obediences. Further, one takes up disciplines only with the guidance of another to help discern the levels appropriate at each given period in one's life. One's trainer should also have been trained in this way, and must not be inclined to force others into his or her personal mold, wanting disciples that think and behave as he or she does. Rather like a good doctor, he or she should be a person who can understand one's unique and real limits, yet who also challenges the

1 Page *xvi*, C. 1982. Paulist Press: 545 Island Road, Ramsey, NJ 07446.

self-imposed limitations that keep one crippled and unable to grow and run freely.

It is certainly possible to grow in this way outside of a monastery, but it is incomparably harder. Those in the world must make some serious choices, or they will be like someone trying to get in shape as a college athlete while living with partying roommates, no goals, schedule or trainer. With guidance and serious effort, however, home life and marriage can become equal challenges and places of disciplined growth in freedom and holiness. Perhaps such an effort will also seem a perversion to many in today's world and even in the Church. Yet to overcome such a perception can be part of the challenge for a serious Christian.

For one touched by the love of God, who sees the vastness of the freedom and joy He has offered us through His own acceptance of the hardship of the Cross, no challenge seems great enough in response. The monastic life, with its challenge to growth on every level, can be a step towards God's eternal freedom and joy.

12

Healing and Monasteries

Men and women come to monasteries for many reasons. The primary reason, the reason for which monasteries have been established, is to welcome those who know they have been touched by God and want to respond by offering Him their whole life. A monastery is meant to be a place where such an offering can be made to God. There, a person having tasted the love of God can seek to empty him or herself of his or her own fallen dreams, ambitions and agendas in order to be filled with the love of Him who alone heals and transforms. All the ascetic disciplines of the monastic life aim at promoting this self-emptying. Thorugh them we seek to "lay aside all earthly cares that we may receive the King of all."[1]

Yet a monastery is not the only place where this can or should be done. Before entering upon the first steps, one must test the community, as St John Climacus says in his *Ladder of Divine Ascent,* to be sure that one will be supervised by doctors and not sick men; that the ship has a pilot and not just ignorant crew members.[2] One who has made this discernment and decided that a certain monastery is indeed where one believes one is to live out this vocation of love and self-denial, must also accept that those who are the guides and teachers in that monastery need to make a similar discernment.

1 Divine Liturgy of St John Chrysostom.
2 *The Ladder of Divine Ascent*, Step 4:6.

Just as a physician must sometimes judge that a very sick person cannot tolerate a certain drug or procedure, so those who have experience in living the monastic life know that certain people who want and need God's healing are far too fragile for strong spiritual medicine. Many such fragile, wounded people come to monasteries. Some seek them on their own. Others are sent by friends or priests who may think that even though they have problems, if they can endure a few rough years they will be straightened out with the help of grace and monastic discipline. They assume that anyone can persevere in a monastery if that is what they want.

Quite frequently, however, wounded people are not at all sure what they want. Usually they have a very distorted view of the monastic life. On the one hand, they hope it will be an escape from a life they have come to find intolerable in the world, and on the other they have real fears of its being a completely unnatural life, not much different from the torture chambers of a concentration camp.

While a magical ability to take deeply disturbed people and have them instantly turn into saints is attributed to monasteries, the asceticism and prayer which have been the traditional means for turning sinners into saints are not popular. Especially in American culture, people perform extreme feats of physical endurance in unquestioning obedience to trainers for the sake of sports, the exploration of outer space, or a simple return to a "natural life-style." Yet far too often a much milder discipline is questioned as an aspect of the monastic life, or even of parish life.

At least part of the reaction against asceticism may be because far too often disciplines have been uniformly imposed without discernment of personal, God-given needs and calling. Such arbitrary imposition of rules comes very close to the binding of burdens too hard to bear that the Lord condemned in the pharisaical practice of His day.[3] Such an approach is far different from supporting another person in growing into what God desires, with the recognition that this differs for each one.

For example, the basic ascetic discipline of obedience, if rightly understood, is a great safeguard against personal whims becoming one's private religion. Yet a person in authority must exercise great discernment in the obedience he or she requests from others. Most people today, even if they do not seem to be deeply troubled or wounded, must begin the path of the ascetic life by practicing voluntary acceptance of the ordinary problems and difficulties of daily life. They should practice giving up their attachment to resentments, bitterness, the taking of offense at any questioning of their words or behavior. They should begin cultivating gratitude and take up the old practice of counting one's blessings daily. Only then can they even think of beginning to undertake the silence and solitude, the prayer, fasting and other forms of self-denial that are the basic monastic medicines for the sickness of self-will and resistance to God and His love. Only those schooled in such forms of self-denial are able to accept, as further medicine, sufferings like those that many endure today in prison camps, war zones, or areas struck by natural disaster, poverty and famine. To endure such suffering without voluntary acceptance does not lead to growth in love and grace, but only to bitterness and further wounding.[4]

Beginners in the Christian journey have a faith far too weak to look upon any unpleasant situation, much less endure it themselves, without jumping to the conclusion that, at least

3 See for example Matthew 23:1-15.
4 *The Ladder Of Divine Ascent* by St John Climacus outlines a classic, monastic asceticism and an unusually punishing one, yet read his warning in Step 4:42.

in this case, God has made a mistake. Yet full Christian faith knows that God does not make mistakes; His "computer" does not slip. Everything, even our own sins and the evil done to us and to others, is part of the reality He has called into being and uses to work out His ultimate good purpose. This is why Orthodox Christians insist that the saving passover into the eternal kingdom of God from this world of sin and suffering was achieved only by God's own suffering in Jesus as He hung upon the Cross.

This is also the reason for the strong tradition that the monastic life is a way to embrace voluntarily, in union with Jesus Christ, an authentic form of living martyrdom. The Lord's words, for example, that "He who would be a disciple of mine must take up his cross daily and follow me"[5] and St Paul's dying daily to the sinful self that he might be alive to Christ,[6] are at the heart of the Gospel message. Men and women in all walks of life have been made saints—have received healing and God's eternal life—in no other way than through accepting suffering in faith, while trusting themselves entirely to Him.

Sometimes monastic community life, in an attempt to help those who come, lost and wounded, can turn into a non-ascetic, "therapeutic" environment. Indeed, many of the people who came and then left over the years have been greatly helped by monasteries through the grace of God. In the process, however, communities often come to realize that they cannot be the ones to help people who are not capable of digesting strong monastic medicine. Such beginners need special programs appropriate for them. Yet these programs may compromise community members' own necessary efforts to live the monastic life. They may sometimes even tempt them to become merely psychological rather than spiritual trainers for those whose faith is not

5   Matthew 16:24.
6   Romans 6:11.

strong enough to accept the tools of ascetic, spiritual healing that are a monastery's heritage.

If a community does feel called to work with people who need such pre-monastic, therapeutic experience, it should be understood that this experience is not training for the life of the community. Such experience is primarily a chance to go back and grow up normally through some of the stages people went through earlier in harmful and damaging ways. A very large part of growing up is finally leaving home or getting pushed out of the nest. Since the point almost always comes when leaving the community is the healthy next step for such men and women, such experience is better sought before attempting to leave home and parish life for a monastery.

While the monastic life is sometimes regarded as a higher and therefore more desirable vocation, if God has something else in mind for a person's life, being turned away from monastic life may lead that person to what is for them a higher calling.

Christian marriage and family are not easy vocations in our world, and they are badly needed. Only parents who are struggling to grow in God's love and the faith of the Church can raise children to be healthy men and women. Workplaces, not to mention homes and parishes, badly need the influence of Christians who are trying to bring God's love and discernment into every word and action of their lives. Indeed, only such families and parishes can prepare men and women for the monastic life.

God may, in His providence, have allowed the damage in the lives of some people who may be too wounded for family life or the workplace and be incapable of living with others in community, because He has something else in mind for them, too.

An extreme illustration of this may be found in the lives of some of the "Fools for Christ." A few people who have been exceptionally sane and healthy, with the advice and consent of their spiritual fathers, have taken on the exterior aspects of insanity as a form of asceticism in an attempt to go beyond the purely social ego.[7] Some, however, seem to have been mentally or emotionally damaged people living in situations where no source of healing could be found for their state; where the Lord withheld the power to cast out the demons and leave them "clothed and in their right minds."[8] Some of them, by accepting the circumstances of their lives, have reached a real holiness. It has also been to the credit of some of those around them that although they might not have had the skills or tools to bring them healing, they have been able to include them in their society with care, compassion and even veneration.

Much will be expected from those who, through no merit of their own, have been given more capacity to grow and enter into God's healing salvation. Those who see themselves as having been given lesser talents must in their turn learn to be faithful in little here in this life, in order to be accounted worthy of the fullness of healing and life in the Kingdom. Whether or not we are following the monastic way, may we be given the strength gradually to grow into an acceptance of the limitations of our lives as well as the suffering and the cross we are asked to carry. With the saints, may we come to embrace these eagerly and joyfully. May we see that the evil, sin and suffering around us and in our own lives can be voluntarily accepted through love and become the means of healing unto eternal life in God's kingdom of love.

7 For a fuller treatment of this subject see the introduction to Vladimir Lossky's, *The Mystical Theology of the Eastern Church* (Crestwood, NY: St Vladimir's Seminary Press,1976).
8 Mark 5:15, Luke 8:35.

13

Building Community

Fallen human beings cannot build community. We want to dispute or ignore such a statement, but we cannot alter the fact and its reality. It is also a fact of human life that we want community: it is a longing that is built into our very nature. So why do our efforts so often encounter blank walls of resistance or create new divisions?

Alexander Solzhenitysn is often quoted as saying "Men have forgotten God." This is true, and it certainly is at the heart of many of the more disastrous attempts by men to build community. Communism has become a byword to us owing to its destructive and futile effort to create a community for mankind without God.

Yet to say that we are going to include God in our community-building efforts is hardly much better. Much of this sort of community building has been done in the name of religious institutions: we are graciously going to allow God to be on our side; we will use His name to justify our pettiness, our quarrels, fights and wars; we will have teachings about His nature, laws about reverence for Him in our daily lives and rubrics to govern the worship that is His due, and we will use all of these as yardsticks to measure each person and decide whether or not they are good enough for the community we are building.

Such a religious attempt by fallen man to build community can, in subtle ways, be even more devastating than efforts to build a community without God, since it has many of the externals that do in fact belong to true community but uses them in ways that betray their real meaning and purpose.

So how is community built? The answer is very simple. What we like to call building community can take place only when we recognize that true community only exists in God. Our job is to enter into it—to enter into His life and make the life, love and energy that are the heart of the Trinity our own life, love and energy. We cannot build true, Christian community by beginning with human plans and agendas for what we and other people are going to do. We have to learn to pray. We need prayer that is more than liturgical worship, though it certainly includes that, but is also our daily and hourly heartfelt cry to God to have mercy on us sinners and to bring us into the life of Jesus Christ.

But here is the rub. We honestly do not believe this. The words of the previous paragraph are rhetoric that good Orthodox Christians will always use when they are called to write essays on building community. If we are totally honest, (and total honesty is one of the prerequisites for true prayer), we will look at how we go about our daily lives and admit that we are functional atheists. We work on saying our prayers, but we know, in our brainwashed, American-dream hearts, that this is just a matter of pious practice and personal discipline. We are convinced that God won't really change us or the people and situations around us. We believe He can, but we know He won't. We need to keep our personal prayer and times of silent listening before Him to a minimum, so we can make space for the real business of rolling up our sleeves and getting to work to fix things ourselves.

Why is this? I can only speak as a 20th century American. I think we Americans add a few twists to Mr. Solzhenitysn's "Men have forgotten God." We would have to qualify this and say that we have forgotten the true, living God. We do in fact keep with us a god of our own making who incarnates many of the traditional religious and theological formulas we have inherited and who is enshrined in our Orthodox Church buildings. And we make sure he stays there, letting us go about the business of setting straight the world that God the Father of Jesus Christ has allowed to turn into a disaster.

In addition, I think we have to say that we have totally forgotten heaven. Historians can trace how this happened in America. Our founding fathers often saw America as the new promised land, the heavenly Jerusalem. We honestly believe that we must create heaven on earth, and that we can do it if only we try hard enough. When it doesn't work, we can always blame God and other people, of course... And we let ourselves get tied up in despairing knots, since if we cannot save the situations we see here and now, we feel as if it were the end of the world.

And we are right. Thank God. Where there is death, there is hope. Paradoxically, only as men and women let go of their attempts to create utopian communities, parishes, jurisdictions, national churches—even countries and brave new worlds—is God able to allow His loving and creative will to be done even here. Even here from time to time, when we will let Him, He can give us a glimpse of what community will be like when we, too, have died; when we have joined our parents, friends, and the thousands upon thousands of righteous men and women who have struggled before us and now watch us (no doubt with some patient amusement) in our struggles here to prove to ourselves that our present life is all that matters. If we will, God will allow them also to become a part of our life, but this will happen only as we accept the fact that heaven will never be made on our terms. To accept this here and now is to begin the first steps of building community that will last into eternal life.

14

Work and Obedience

The garden of Eden, in the mind of fallen man, has come to be equated with unrestrained pleasure, idyllic ease and, last but not least, the tantalizing hope that temptation is just around the corner. Why, then, do monastics, who are notorious for turning their backs on pleasure and temptation and for working very hard, often say that their life is in large part an attempt to return to the state of mankind in Paradise?

"The Lord God took the man and put him in the garden of Eden to till it and keep it."[1] It is a Biblical intuition that work is the first calling of humanity, more basic even than social life. Yet it was work in a certain context, in a garden where all was in harmony with its Creator, where Adam himself lived with a sense of purpose and trust. He had not yet been tempted to create his own agenda apart from what he could do best by nature and calling. He and God were able to listen to one another, hear and see one another without fear or shame. As God beheld Adam, He saw that more was needed, that it was not good for man to be alone. He added the context of a society of animals, and finally of a person who was like Adam yet different enough to be seen as other.

This was an idyllic situation, including, not in spite of, the work. Surrounded by beauty and harmony, knowing he was doing what he could do best, having the love and trust of those around him and the security of knowing his all-good and all-powerful Creator, Adam had the energy needed to meet

1 Genesis 2:15.

each day with joy and the excitement of discovery. Sickness, death and sorrow were not yet in his vocabulary.

There are those even now who would be happy to find themselves in such a paradise, who can prefer its joys and delights to the destructive pleasures of fallen man. Most of us, however, fall somewhere in between. We know we should prefer the delights of paradise, and at times we do even enjoy being good, but there are pleasures that we see are doing harm to ourselves and others that we are not ready to give up. We try to hide from God in what we may perceive as just a small, harmless rebellion. We often prefer to have even other people at a distance so that we can forget their love and not be reminded that we have an alternative to our private, destructive behaviors.

We try to excuse ourselves, as Adam and Eve did when they chose to trade paradise for fallen pleasure. We blame everyone, from God on down, for the choices we continue to make each day.

And it is true that others may help us along the way into our private hell. The evil active in the serpent is a vicious, personal being, nursing eternal hatred and envy for God. His unending resentment and malice drive him to seduce others away from the joys of paradise and infect them with the same passion of seductive hatred and rebellion against all that is good, true and beautiful.

Although we are trapped in this battlefield of evil, sometimes not understanding that we are fighting on the side of the enemy as often as we fight on the side of love and truth, moments come to each of us when we see clearly that we do have choices. In such moments, we recognize the love that is of God, whether we experience it as a direct revelation from Him or as coming through people and events around us. This comes with what may be the shattering discovery of how much He loves us, and how much others share in His love for us.

However it may come, such a moment brings us to the point of a decision. Having seen true love and beauty, we understand that we no longer have to settle for the pleasures we had enjoyed but now see are false and deceptive. Even if we do not want it wholeheartedly yet, we see that we can choose to do what is necessary to return to the state of Adam in the true paradise of God. And instinctively we know that whatever else this may mean, it is going to mean work.

Our first job—and we will find that it is very hard work—is to learn to turn to God, to try to listen to Him, to pray. If we are in earnest, He will lead us to the people, the books, the experiences we need.

In this work of prayer, we will need to search out the wisdom and riches of the Church. Monastics are truly blest to have great riches at their disposal. For several hours every day they undertake what has been called the Work of God: chanting and listening with attention to the Psalms and other Scriptures of the Church, the writings of the Fathers, lives of the saints, hymns and prayers. For fallen human beings, this can be indeed very hard work.

People who are able to stand for hours in long lines to buy tickets to baseball games or concerts, jog for miles and work out in a gym may find that it is nearly impossible to stand even for a few minutes paying attention to something other than their own ideas and feelings and the music and noise of the world. Yet people living in the world with jobs and families must also take on this work to a greater or lesser degree. Even when it is not possible to attend extra church services, they can say the Lord's prayer with attention at least once daily, although preferably twice, in the morning and the evening. It is good to use the Trisagion prayers of the Church in some regular way, and Psalms when possible. It is best to have a set time and place for this: the time, a few minutes before family chores in the morning, the place, an icon corner in a room. If those in the house and at work are hostile and prayers must be hidden, one can always lock oneself into a bathroom at home or at work for a few minutes in order to pray in this way. Even in monasteries people must struggle with their priorities and work to be present for prayer.

We, no less than the Christians of the early Church, are attempting to throw down the idols we have been worshipping, including our own ego and opinions, not to mention worldly goods, power, money and prestige. We must challenge and cut out the rituals we use religiously to keep us tied to these and to other false supports such as addicting substances, behaviors and relationships. We must begin to do this, placing the true God and Creator in His rightful place at the center of our life. We must use the ritual and service He has inspired through thousands of years of His self-revelation to Israel and His Church. But then we will find our old, fallen habits taking on a life of their own and challenging us in return with a strength that can only be called demonic. To persevere in this work of God can mean a heroic struggle and will call us to develop a discipline at least as far reaching as any effort directed towards a worldly goal.

Moreover, the work of discipline, by definition, means becoming a disciple. This means, first of all, a disciple of Christ. Yet, then, one comes to realize that those who do not love those around them whom they can see cannot love God whom they do not see.[2] This love includes respect and the desire and willingness to learn how others think and act. Someone who is not willing to be taught by others, to search out those who have gained experience by working longer in this way and follow their example, is not truly willing to be taught by and to follow God.

2 Cf. 1 John 4:20-21.

Becoming a disciple is a start towards learning to work in the same context in which Adam worked. We must conquer the fallen self, the ego, with its false sense of identity. In order to regain our God-given identity, to do and be what He created us to do and be, we must first learn to do things as others do them, putting aside our own ideas, opinions and ways. This can be very difficult. It is like waging war against the very root of our sense of self. This warfare is at the heart of all monastic life with its obedience.

Before we are able to take on the voluntary, all-encompassing obedience of a monastery, however, most of us begin by waging small, involuntary battles. We may see, for example, that in order to keep a job it is important to do things the way the boss wants them done rather than the way we would do them if we were on our own. We may do this grudgingly, from a sense of compulsion, but gradually find ourselves growing into a greater freedom as we realize that now we are not limited to doing things our way. We can also do them another way. If our boss is a wise, experienced person, we may begin to realize in addition that his or her way is better than ours or at least teaches us things we had not known before about our work. We begin to realize that our sense of worth has not been diminished, but that now others are looking at us with greater respect, as more experienced. We learn that by putting aside our limited experience to learn from the experience of others we can grow more than we have ever been able to grow before.

Over the years, we learn to do many things we would never have dreamed possible on our own. We discover capabilities we never thought we had. As we grow in love and trust of those around us, with greater respect for the way they do things, we find our prayer deepens and we are able to have more of a sense that God is providing direction in our whole life. With the help and discernment of others, we come to see that there are tasks given to us in God's providence that no one else can do. We are able to serve more selflessly with the love and support of others in these God-given tasks.

We also find we have more energy as we lose the need to maintain our own interests and agendas, and we gradually become more aware of the world around us. We are able to work much harder, no matter what our task may be. No longer centered on our self, we seek out God's creation, wanting to see it as He sees it. Other people, different from our friends, become interesting to us, and we want to learn their ways as well. Nature, the earth, animals, plants all have a new claim on our life.

If we follow this way to the end, after our death we will find ourselves entering paradise and rejoicing to see the fulfillment of God's creation around us. Surrounded by the saints gathered from all peoples, nations and languages, by not only the rest of the visible creation we have known but also by the angels, archangels, principalities and powers we cannot see on this earth, we will discover that we have more than recovered the state of Adam in paradise. We have entered into the fullness of the stature of Christ and found universal joy and peace in the eternal work of praise in heaven.

15

Martyrdom and the Vision of God

The word "martyr" has fallen on bad times. "You don't want to be a martyr, do you?" is not an uncommon question in late 20th-century America, and "No" is the obvious answer. It is hard to believe that there were centuries during which average Christians in reasonable states of psychological health replied without hesitation: "I do!" Most of us today would have to think twice and do some mental gymnastics to give such a positive reply.

What has happened? Has the meaning of the word "martyr" changed? The word "martyr" in English derives from the Greek word *martys*, meaning witness. In the early Church, this word came to have a technical meaning: witness to the Gospel truth of God in Christ. Even as late as the mid-20th century, this was still the primary English dictionary definition. In this particular usage, apart from the vision of God in Christ, there is no true martyrdom or witness, only false witness. Jesus Himself is referred to in the scriptures as "the true witness."

Our present use of the English word martyr, however, reflects the culture around us. Our society no longer has a Christian vision of God, and since the word martyr also has lost its connection with the root meaning of witness, it no longer reflects the Christian definition. But our society does have a great deal of despair, sickness, depression, anxiety and negativity, and they are the content of the meaning now connected with the word martyr. When we hear about or speak of martyrs, we tend to think of people who are suffering for all the wrong reasons: spineless, sick people, for example, who allow their alcoholic spouses to abuse them. Whether or not they are actually killed in the situation, we often say such people have a "martyred air": they are joyless, have a chronic attitude of reproachful resentment and are unwilling to take responsibility for their own lives. This is a complete reversal of the joy, hope and courage that are the hallmarks of true Christian martyrs.

Some other uses of the word also confuse the issue for us. When a saintly Christian has been killed in circumstances that do not clearly indicate a challenge to the faith, the Church has debated whether he or she could technically be called a martyr. A category of "passion-bearers" has arisen, particularly in the Russian Church, for those who are killed for political or other motives and meet their death in Christ's own spirit of love and forgiveness. Holiness takes many forms, and not everyone is given the grace to die because he or she proclaims Jesus Christ as Lord and God. Today, the common usage of the word martyr for those who die from AIDS, for example, is likewise problematic. If someone were sentenced to a slow death for refusing to deny his or her belief in Christ by being given an injection of HIV positive blood, yes, he or she would die as a martyr. Those who die from AIDS in an innocent, Christian manner, may well be venerated as passion-bearers. We have compassion and pray for those who suffer and die for any reason, even in spirits other than love, joy, peace and self-control, but we can ask ourselves what witness their death gives? We are free to die for all sorts of things—a great love for chocolate, cigarettes, or climbing mountains. But such deaths are not Christian martyrdom.

How can we regain the spirit of joy and eager readiness for martyrdom that characterizes Christians even in our own century in places such as the former Soviet Union? We used the term "mental gymnastics" earlier—perhaps that bears some closer scrutiny. Our minds do not think as Christian minds should. In classic terms, we need to repent. In the Gospels, this English word translates the Greek *metanoia*, which means a change not only in our mind but our entire attitude. First we need to admit that we are sinners. Yet see how we can manage to twist even this admission of our sinfulness. Many of us find it easy to admit that we are sinners. We repeat to ourselves that we are sinners, reinforcing our sinful behavior. We may even boast that we are sinners, feeling at least that this means we are not hypocrites.

Yet in Christ's reality, to say I am a sinner means something very different. It means that I take responsibility for my life, my thoughts, words, actions and behavior. In modern terms, it means I have hit bottom and am finally willing to change. It means I admit that I alone am living my life and that I have made a mess of it. No one else can live it for me or force me to sin. Often in Orthodox hymnody we find such phrases as "I, I alone have sinned." These are powerful statements. Unless I am an infant or severely brain damaged, I cannot blame anyone else or the situations around me for my responses. They are mine and I choose to make them. To admit to being a sinner in this sense is the only way I can begin to show the fruits of repentance, the only way I can begin to live in the power and love of Christ. God does not enslave us as sins, passions and demons do. Only when we freely take responsibility for our lives and choose to change does God freely live and act within us.

How important it is for us to repent in this way. To be able to do so is true grace from God. Only by this grace and by God's living His own life within us can we begin to have the vision of God. The true vision of God is not some imaginative picture of Jesus sitting on a cloud next to His bearded Father.

The true vision of God sees reality as it comes from God. It sees much further than our extremely limited human vision. It sees within, to the depths of both the wonder of our created being and the horror of our chosen sin. It sees beyond, to the eternal life that is ours with Christ, tasted for brief moments on this earth and realized fully in paradise. It sees the glory of Christ, not only in His earthly wisdom and miracles, but most especially when He dies on the Cross in agony for all the sin and tragedy of His fallen creation. People who see in this way begin to love. They begin to understand that they would not trade God's reality in Christ for anything, that they would be willing even to die for such truth and beauty. They begin to understand that beyond this world and beyond physical death there is eternal life, without sin and tragedy, that they can only guess at here.

Now we can begin true mental gymnastics. We can begin to focus our lives, to use St Paul's comparison, in the same way competing athletes do. Not to win an Olympic medal, but to win the crown of eternal life. We can begin to take time each day to place ourselves consciously in the presence of God, in the presence of holy things such as the icons of the Church. We can begin to fill our minds with words and thoughts of reality—not all the negative, hopeless, depressed thoughts we have programmed into our brains and that we habitually reinforce, but the true words of hope, salvation, confidence, strength and joy we find in the Scriptures, the prayers, the liturgical services of the Church and the lives and writings of the saints. We can focus on the Kingdom of God, our true mission and goal in life. The Lord said that we do not need to be anxious for food, clothing, or a good salary. He has told us to let others be anxious for those things if they so desire. God knows we need them, and we can save our energy for what is really necessary. When we seek God's Kingdom and His righteousness first of all, everything else will be given to us as well, including the ability to do our necessary work. We can begin to respect ourselves as made in the image and likeness of God and reject all false martyrdoms, as the Lord Himself walked away from abuse when His time had not yet come.

The monastic life has often been referred to as a "white martyrdom." We pray that our own life may indeed be such a witness. As we go on our annual Lenten journey to Pascha may we beg God for the grace of His vision. May we be allowed to live in the spirit of true Christian martyrdom, whether or not we are allowed to die a martyr's death. May we greet one another now and into eternity with the Paschal words: "Christ is Risen!"

16

Persons

Who am I? On a beautiful spring day in the country, when the sun is shining and the birds are singing, I am fit, in every sense of that word. I forget about myself and know I am literally in place; belonging to the beauty around me.

That sense of total belonging never lasts for long. Unlike the warm rock on which I sit, I must get up and move on. While I live, I cannot lie there passively for millennia being warmed or frozen through summer and winter, eroded and crumbled into the soil that surrounds me. Nor can I be as rooted as the ferns and trees, the grasses and wildflowers. Even the birds and animals in the woods around me are part of the fabric of this place in a way that I am not. They cannot create their own artificial environment elsewhere and survive in it as I can. Destroy this place and they will be gone; capture them and they will die.

And yet I know there should be something similar in my own life: "Look at the birds of the air: they neither sow nor reap nor gather into barns, and yet your heavenly Father feeds them. Are you not of more value than they? ...Consider the lilies of the field, how they grow; they neither work nor spin. Yet I tell you Solomon in all his glory was not arrayed like one of these. But if God so clothes the grass of the field, which today is alive and tomorrow is thrown into the fire, will he not much more clothe you, O men of little faith?"[1]

1 Matthew 6:26-30.

I find it hard to believe it is that simple. I am in a universe governed by seemingly random tragedy. The placid, sunny sky above me opens out to seemingly infinite space, filled with black holes ready to suck in whole galaxies, stars and suns, planets, moons and comets that also explode, burn out and collide. The planet earth is not at all solid or stable. Whole continents collide. They are riddled with volcanoes ready to pile molten debris over me, while earthquakes can pull the ground out from under me. The weather scours landscapes down to bare rocks with wind and rain or burns everything in sight with drought and fire. Even when the earth seems to be at rest, the warm rocks, the grass and trees, birds and animals that give me a sense of peaceful belonging depend on one organism's survival through the destruction of another. Even the life-giving soil on which I stand is teeming with bacteria, worms and insects busily devouring dirt and one another day in and day out.

I see again the similarity with my own life. Am I simply one more random part of this earth and this universe, driven by forces seemingly no more personal than a volcano or a hurricane? Is this ability to reflect, and the attempt to capture such reflection in words, a macabre joke? Is what I call myself a meaningless by-product of consciousness trapped in a vast, unconscious system of time and space?

"...God created Adam in His own image, in the image of God He created him; male and female He created them."[2] Part of us knows we are something more than an aberrant part of an impersonal whole. Through the millennia since we were inspired to lurch our bodies upright and begin the process leading to modern humanity, we have sensed communication with life beyond what we can touch and see. Through revelation we have met the personal love that created this universe and has been

2   Genesis 1:27.

reaching out, waiting and brooding over the life of this world, until we also live and love in personal response. We have come to know a reality far more wonderful than any contemporary fantasy world of science fiction, an eternity of life so full and abundant that our seemingly infinite universe of time and space is a drop in the ocean by comparison. While we may see this love as in a hazy mirror, it is no mistake that we recognize its image. All of us together, young and old, healthy and infirm, rich and poor, male and female, yellow, black, white and red, from every continent on earth, are Adam, even though now we are born deformed with fallen flesh, outside the gates of paradise. Yet each one of us is also a unique creation by and in the image and likeness of this Love.

The image and likeness of the Life we dare to call our God, means freedom—the freedom even to refuse or destroy our freedom. The evil, destructive side of creation that seems to be an equal part of us, seems also to force on us the capacity to deny our own personal spirit, to take our own life, or to refuse to grow beyond the life of an animal made from the dust.

Since the revelation of life in Jesus, Christians have identified these two tendencies with the "old" and the "new" Adam—Adam being simply the Hebrew word for mankind. In the tradition found in Genesis, the old Adam, made from dust, yet in the image and likeness of God, was tempted by evil and death in the person of the devil and fell to become his slave along with the rest of creation. The new Adam is refashioned in the image and likeness of God incarnate in Christ Jesus, who destroys evil and death by his own innocent death, raises our humanity in Himself and lifts it up to the level of eternal creative love, the right hand of the Father in heaven.

Our whole life reflects the struggle between these two natures. Instead of freely being real persons in the image and likeness of God by accepting our God-given potential and worth, as

well as the limitations of our fallen, sin-ridden nature, we identify our personality with a false ego based on a fantasy image we
have invented of who we are and what we would like to be.
Such a pseudo-personality is easily humiliated.

The truly humble person, however, simply cannot be humiliated: he knows fallen human nature for what it is, including his
own particular limitations, and is never surprised at his own sins
and failings. Nor do these sins and failings cause him to doubt
himself in the eyes of God. Rather than leading him to despair
since once again he has failed and therefore is not the person he
wants to be, he is able to turn to God with renewed faith and
trust that God, his Creator, will do in him what he, by his own
fallen efforts, cannot. Nor is he shattered by destructive events
and situations around him, beyond his control. Again, knowing
his own limitations, he realizes that only God comprehends the
whole of reality, that the seeming triumph of the forces of evil
and destruction in this world are only the death agony of an order that is passing away. Even when his perceptions may seem
to contradict him, he has learned to turn to God, knowing that
His triumph in the Resurrection of Christ is worthy of ultimate
faith, hope, love and trust.

Such turning toward God, to use St Paul's image, in order
to see ourselves however dimly in that mirror,[3] is the only true
basis for understanding ourselves, for understanding human
personality and our ultimate destiny beyond this world. Turning toward God is the only true meaning of the word prayer. It
is the way we can begin to overcome our convenient forgetful-
ness of who we truly are. We can begin to stop playing God in
our own lives, as well as in the lives of others and in the world
around us. We can come to see that God does not play at life as
we do even as adults, behaving like destructive and demanding

3   1 Corinthians 13:12.

two-year old tyrants. By prayer we can begin rather to be persons and to love in God's way by having mercy, denying ourselves, taking up our cross daily and laying down our life for our friends.[4]

4 Luke 9:23ff.

17

Christian Celibacy

Monks and nuns have always had to struggle to come to terms with their vocation. Celibacy is often a large part of that struggle, since few people simply choose celibacy as a life style. The conscious choice of most people is to be married and to have children. Yet Christians who consider themselves to be part of the normal order of things, preparing themselves for a life of marriage and family as they grow up, sometimes also come to experience another call. They may hear the words of the Lord in the Gospel describing those who have "left house or wife or brothers or parents or children, for the sake of the kingdom of God,"[1] or the words of St Paul saying, "The unmarried woman or virgin is anxious about the affairs of the Lord, how to be holy in body and spirit; but the married woman is anxious about worldly affairs, how to please her husband. I say this for your own benefit, not to lay any restraint upon you, but...to secure your undivided devotion to the Lord."[2] They sense that the Holy Spirit is speaking these words to them. They may sense a personal challenge and invitation to follow the Lord in a way they had not before thought to be possible.

And this may bring them to a real struggle. A woman entering monastic life may feel that there is a large part of herself that says she cannot be a nun; God made her to be married and have children, how could He be asking her to give

1 Luke 18:29.
2 1 Corinthians 7:34-35.

this up? She knows Him as a God of love: what is this strange kind of love that He is trying to teach her?

Working through this struggle is truly at the heart of a healthy celibacy, we believe. This is because to side-step it in any way means failing to grasp the depth of the reality God has given us, including our nature as sexual beings. And unless we understand this, we will not be prepared for the depth and intensity of the struggle we will have to face. Non-monastics often seem to consider the stories from the Desert Fathers, for example, of the monks and nuns struggling against sexual temptations to be "out of proportion" or signs of perversion. They sometimes take this to mean that they should not have become monks and nuns in the first place. No. If one becomes a monk or a nun, one had better be prepared for the massive battle that lies ahead, because it is a challenge; it can seem to cut at the very heart of what it means to be a human being.

Married people need to come to terms with this struggle also, or they will be incapable of friendships outside of their marriage and sometimes even of healthy relationships with their own growing children. If they have never really grappled with loving without sexual expression, and do not want to deal with the struggle that comes with facing temptation as temptation, when they do form a friendship and sexual feelings come up—especially in this day and age—they figure they either should give up the relationship, have an affair, or else get divorced and remarried. The alternative of seeing the sexual feelings as temptations that can and must be fought against, conquered and overcome often does not even appear as a possibility. They *can* seem to tear one apart at the very center of one's being. Yet no matter how powerful they are, they must be seen as temptations precisely for the sake of love, and love for one's neighbor as well as for God. This is true even though in this life they will always return to begin the war again.

The whole point of the Christian ascetic life is to train us to love even when it is not easy. It is easy to feel we are loving when in fact we do not care at all about God or the other person, and are driven only by our selfish desires and needs. We must work toward self-denial in love by gradually taking on fasting and abstinence under obedience, as training in this warfare. We need discipline to restrain our self-serving, fallen possessiveness and instead allow the love that is of God to reach out through us to others. We must learn to pray so that His great love fills our lives and strengthens us.

Perhaps the struggle is even greater today. The "media" put out such an assault, blatantly trying to "turn people on" with music, suggestion, explicit pictures—most advertising today seems to be pornographic—so that one simply cannot pass through society today as an untouched innocent. One does not have to have been married and/or "had sex" to be "turned on" and have to struggle with temptation on that level. Even if one chooses to avoid such temptation, it is impossible to do so. Go to the dentist, and suggestive music is blaring over the radio. Make a phone call to straighten out an electric bill, and you have to listen to the same thing while they put you on hold. Get a prescription filled at the drugstore, and you have to see a display for condoms.

And again the struggle is not essentially different for married couples. While sex is blessed as a normal part of marriage, there is certainly more to marriage than this. People sometimes say St John of Kronstadt was not really married. It is not that simple. His wife, Catherine, had a hard time at first, not understanding and accepting after their marriage that her husband did not want them to sleep together but to live as brother and sister. But she came to accept this wholeheartedly. They did have a marriage and became very close, even physically. After he died she would wrap herself in his coat to feel his presence.

They lived together; they just did not "have sex." And we know of a couple who found out that the husband is HIV positive from a blood transfusion and has developed AIDS. Because he does not want to infect his wife, and because there is no way of having completely "safe sex," they have stopped sleeping together. They are traveling and giving talks together, and they say it has deepened their marriage and their love for each other and feel it is important to say this, that there is an alternative to sex and, yes, there is life after AIDS.

This also helps us to understand how God works in our lives through His providence. He does not make mistakes. Nothing happens that He has not foreseen and allowed, and that does not work for our salvation. This is true even if we can see it only as the death of all that we know to be good, beautiful and saving, as was the crucifixion of Jesus. There are people who seem to think it would have been much better if Jesus had been able to live longer, perhaps even marry, and die a peaceful death. Given such thinking, if one's spouse dies, or if the relationship does not grow as one hoped or expected, or if "Mr. Right" never comes along for one to marry in the first place—how can one help but become bitter, frustrated and resentful? After all, one is a normal person, meant to have a meaningful, interdependent relationship with a member of the opposite sex. The Lord obviously was not speaking about them, they feel, when he said there can be no extra-marital sex, or divorce, or remarriage, without sin for those involved. And that only hardness of heart would allow such sin. They seem unable to acknowledge themselves as responsibile in these relationships.

No, fornication and adultery are not the unforgivable sin. It is obvious from the Scriptures that the Lord did not intend His teaching on marriage to give those who abuse their spouses and children unlimited power over them. Yes, the Church in pastoral reality allows penitential re-marriage for lay people. But today few even see the need for the penitence. It is seen only as a step in the right direction to get out of a dishonest, sexless or "love-less" relationship and into one that is "meaningful." Therefore it is regarded as the opposite of sin. The need for physical sex becomes perhaps the most powerful addiction and many people are incapable of considering the possibility of a relationship without it. Their reasons for continuing with an illicit affair when it goes against even their own sense of what is good and true seem to be of the same kind as the reasons for continuing to smoke or drink inappropriately. Tragically, such people undermine their own integrity and self esteem, especially if they have the sense that their relationship is not based on anything that would continue if they stopped having sex.

Monastics are often equated with the workaholic whose addictive approach to a career or a cause deadens his or her sexual appetite. It is true that they need to work and keep busy, but this can become, like even the misuse of the Jesus prayer, a way of avoiding issues that should be faced. Monastic literature considers such addictive attachment to work and ambition to be the opposite of asceticism and as destructive to the life as active fornication.

When we are really following Jesus, no addictive behavior can be justified or condoned. Instead, we seek freedom and the joy that it alone can bring: freedom to love others as Christ has loved, the strength to lay down our life for our friends, to turn the other cheek, walk the next mile, or wash the feet of our brethren. But where faith is not so strong and our Christianity has been diluted or distorted by other agendas, we can imagine like Dostoyevsky's Grand Inquisitor, that we are doing a good thing by ignoring what Jesus taught. Understanding the radical nature of what Jesus was saying—about love, marriage, work, possessions—was, in earlier history, what converted our civilization. But that conversion has been turned inside out now, so that our society's values are no longer those of Jesus but of the Prince of this world. Once again, Christians are faced with hard choices that may cause society to scorn or even remove them if they live their faith with integrity. Celibacy—Christian chastity—is certainly on the front lines of this struggle.

18

Human Love

Part 1: American Style

"Love and marriage
go together like a horse and carriage.
You just ask your mother:
you can't have one without the other!"

So began a popular song that Americans heard in the 1950's. Most young people, especially girls, sang it with a warm, virtuous feeling. They were not "bad." They would not do any of "those things" until they got married. They all knew some girls who did "those things," but they were in the minority, and "most people" realized young women "had a problem" if they behaved that way; that "bad" boys took advantage of them, and that such boys and girls should be sent away to get themselves straightened out.

As the 60's moved in, though, the warm, virtuous feeling faded. Young people, confronted by adult reality, seemed to see all their dreams and ideals shattered and were left instead with feelings of anger, tension and frustration. Those who went on to "higher education" would find themselves listening to professors who would tell them, in the name of "mental hygiene" that these feelings were not healthy (that rang a bell) and that they could be dealt with most constructively through the outlet of physical sex. They were informed that they should look upon what was once equated with love and marriage as a normal function, like sneezing, which would make them feel better when they were out of sorts. Whatever brought the best results (i.e. the quickest response) could be used: another person of whichever sex you preferred, or self-stimulation in the privacy of your own room. Many found that drugs, food, alcohol and even some approaches to work, play and meditation could be used to obtain the same results. It was all very simple.

They had not encountered a serious concept of love, however, except "that thing" that men and women get to do when they are married. ("You can't have one without the other.") Now "that thing" had been separated from marriage and put into the category of normal, healthy physical functions. While this normal, healthy function might temporarily remove some feelings of anger, tension and frustration, it did not take some people long to discover that it had very little to do with love. Even the brief minutes of experiencing feelings of warm intimacy that might accompany one's encounter with another person or the substance or activity of one's choice could make the remaining long hours, days and years of existence even bleaker. These encounters, in spite of a blossoming "I love _____" bumper-sticker campaign in their support, could not remove an ever-growing sense that there must be something more to loving. Not having many clues as to what this "more" might be, they spent years continuing such encounters, trying different people, sexes, activities and substances, in the hope that someday the right combination would "do the trick." Left with a far deeper feeling of distress and alienation, many came to believe that love had been removed from the universe, or, more probably, had never been there in the first place. Any resistance they might have felt to the philosophy of existence taught in some school science courses was removed once and for all.

Some were fortunate enough to have grown up on farms where nature and the sanity of animals made up for many human failings. Others had families that through inherited cultural (usually what was called "ethnic") habits expressed more love in non-sexual ways. These people could sometimes shake the cobwebs from their brains and get on with loving and living in spite of what they heard and saw around them. Far too many others were raised by parents who, riding the recent wave of human technology and progress produced by the two World Wars of this century, had very little time for anything their children could identify as love. "Performance Orientation" seemed to be the one value esteemed in family life.[1] Being a success in school, sports, work and social life outside the family (including Church activities) was normally the one way to gain attention and approval from others and hence acquire some sort of positive self-image.

Most were aware that their parents had physical, sexual relations with each other and even with other people, but as they saw the divorce rate grow, or found themselves trapped into pathological relationships in the name of wedlock, they realized that even here there was often no love. "The" sexual act even within marriage was not the magic formula for love they had been led to expect.

Religion entered in for some as a way to search for love. This is true in spite of the fact that if they were Roman Catholic, the Second Vatican Council shook the foundations of their most cherished beliefs. Likewise, if they were Protestants and Jews they heard their leaders telling them that God was dead and that service to mankind, not to an impersonal God, was the way to human fulfillment. And if they were Orthodox they were taught almost nothing and understood even less during church services which were frequently in a language even their parents had for-

1 John and Paula Sandford, *The Transformation of the Inner Man* (Tulsa: Victory House, 1982), ch. 3.

gotten. Still, whatever lack of faith they had encountered or misinformation they might have received in the name of religious education, they had all heard at one time or another that "God is love." Their experience as Americans ("In God we trust") with what could only be called a developing civil religion had not given them any clear way to make sense of that statement, but at least it seemed to leave an idealistic use for the word love in their vocabulary.

Through what remained of their childhood good will and enthusiasm, some joined institutions of American civil religion, the Peace Corps or the military. Others went so far as to enter seminaries, Bible schools, monasteries and convents to seek after this vanishing love. Often, however, they found that they were not solving the problems of mankind. Nor were they having a ravishing experience that removed them from this earth and set them safely in the third heaven where all past doubts and experiences could be forgotten. Rather, they found themselves surrounded by people who hated what they were giving them in the name of American generosity, or were trapped in the worst horrors of chemical guerrilla warfare, or found themselves with men and women who even though officially in the Church were experiencing the same doubts and tensions as they did. Ways of expressing affection and friendship which they had learned to distrust if they did not identify themselves as "gay" were especially suspect in celibate religious institutions. ("Love and marriage/...You can't have one without the other.") By the 70's, after years of trying to manufacture artificially some marginal form of love based on books they read, those left in such religious institutions felt that their efforts were like patching a hemorrhaging grenade wound with a small bandaid.

By the end of the 90's, a person transported by a time machine from the 50's or even 60's, would hardly be able to recognize American society and its institutions. Not having participated in the evolutionary process, he would be tempted to think that the country was trapped in a tidal wave of mass insanity. He would point out parallels with Nazi Germany, up to and including legislation allowing society to permit the controlled destruction of certain categories of human life, and the denial either that this is happening or that there might be anything wrong with it if it is.

He would also see that religion has never before reached such heights. Many gods are worshipped with religious devotion. Evocative descriptions of the act of physical sex are inserted religiously in contemporary literature and advertising. Devotion to food and health are hardly less assiduously cultivated and proclaimed through books, media and workshops. The power, worship and wealth offered to the stars of sports, movies and television and the providers of mood-and-mind-altering substances far exceed anything offered to the emperors of Byzantium as God's regents on earth. The buildings erected on behalf of their aggrandizement dwarf earlier shrines such as the British Stonehenge, the pyramids of Egypt and the cathedrals of Europe.

Television and other forms of mass media have ensured that very few people in America have not been drastically affected by this mass religious insanity. Those few have either been locked up in solitary confinement because of their crimes or personal insanity, or through some instinct have chosen a form of voluntary exile, finding or creating a place where they can live apart from society and its "media." Even monasteries, the traditional place to go for a Christian choosing such voluntary exile, have rarely maintained an integrity distinct from this environment. Individuals who through conservatism dislike what they see around them nevertheless frequently adopt the attitude, "If you can't lick 'em, join 'em," providing an even more complex and problematic situation for the authentic American dissident.

Part 2: A Transition

"God is the Lord and has revealed Himself to us!"[2] This statement is the ancient yet ever new Judeo-Christian response and challenge to American mass insanity. It shows the God of revelation reaching out as surely as He has reached out to humanity and the whole of His Creation from the beginning of time in a way that has given full, positive meaning to the statement, "God is love."

The means of His self-revelation are as many as His creatures. "Ever since the creation of the world His invisible nature, namely, His eternal power and deity, has been clearly perceived in the things that have been made."[3] "He is not far from each one of us, for 'in Him we live and move and have our being'; as even some of your poets have said."[4]

It seems that some people have a direct experience of the Living God, whom from that time on they cannot deny no matter how much others may question their sanity, and whom they can only see as the Most Important Person and the Greatest Love in their lives. Others, meeting or hearing of such people and their experience, find themselves in some way entering into that same experience. Many of them would also claim a direct experience of God, mediated through that other person. The situations in which these encounters with the Living God occur are as varied as the people who experience them. Some may be headed into a situation where they plan to act in a certain way, only to find themselves knocked off their high horses and led toward a completely different course of action.[5] Some

2 Psalm 117(118): 27; Septuagint version as used by the Orthodox Church.
3 Romans 1:20.
4 Paul preaching to the men of Athens, Acts 17:27-28.
5 Acts 9:1-22.

may be looking at the early blossoms of a fruit tree, and in that moment be given an overwhelming realization of God's creative and renewing love and reality.[6] Some may be called to read a passage in a book and find their own thoughts interrupted with what they can only call a revelation of God's presence that goes far beyond the meaning of the words before them.[7] Some find themselves seemingly trapped at the end of a one-way, dead-end street, only to experience God's opening to them what seems a new lifetime filled with love.[8]

Here, for the most part, we are speaking of the experience of adults. The Christian Church has canonized many of them as the great penitents. They seemed headed in a certain less than divine direction until their lives were turned around by God and led to a realization of the state they were in. They came to see their need for repentance, forgiveness and healing so that they could respond adequately to Him and reveal to others the great goodness, truth and love He had shown them. These men and women provide the greatest hope for those who see their own lives badly warped by their responses to damaging people or situations. They have left more than an account of their experiences of God for us. Their experience has led them to great wisdom, and their words and writings, their teaching about reality, open up a whole dimension largely lost to human society. They speak of a love that has not left the universe but permeates it and has permeated it from before the dawn of time. They speak of a love vast enough to embrace the far reaches of outer space, yet delicate enough to measure the distances between the bundles of energy that form the atomic

7 "Conversations with Brother Lawrence," *The Practice of the Presence of God*, tr. John J. Delaney (Garden City, NY: Image Books, 1977).

8 Augustine of Hippo, *Confessions* tr. Rex Warner (New York: New American Library, 1963), 182-83.

structure of what we know as material reality. They speak of a love prodigal enough to have spent thousands—millions—of years as if they were mere days preparing the earth before we came into being, not willing for a single sparrow—or dinosaur—to fall without purpose. They speak of this Love revealing itself most fully in the man Jesus, walking among men and teaching them by His words and actions that "Greater love has no man than this: that a man lay down his life for his friends;"[8] that God Himself "so loved the world that He gave His only-begotten Son, so that whoever believes in Him may not perish, but have everlasting life;"[9] that He "did not send His Son into the world to condemn the world, but that through Him the world might be saved."[10]

This is the Love we call human. It is the love that raises men and women above their merely animal instincts. It is a love that possesses an ever-renewed vision of a life without end; a Kingdom not of this world. It is a love that claims to experience that which is beyond human experience, and to transform even the most horrible and seemingly hopeless situations into steps leading to love, freedom and joy. It is a love that claims the ability to face and accept what is true no matter how it presents itself. There have been brief moments in human history when entire families, entire groups of people, have come to participate in this experience of love. Children have been brought into their midst and raised in an atmosphere protected by love, hardly touched by the world's spirit of insanity and despair. Such children grow into adults having a spiritual, mental and emotional health others can only guess at. We would like to guess, though, and from what we know of health, sketch a brief outline of this true human love from the

8   John 15:13.
9   John 3:16.
10 John 3:17.

time of conception to the time of death.

Part 3: Christian Style

Even before such children are conceived, their parents want them, pray for them and hope they will be a result of the ways they share their love for each other. When they discover that they have received the gift of a new life, they rejoice. They pray and work harder than before to make ready. The father and other members of the immediate and extended family do everything within their power to support the mother in her unique role as the only immediate source of all the child's needs. Being cherished by those about her, the mother knows she and her baby are loved and cared for, safe and secure. She delights in having it grow so intimately within her. Wherever she is, she realizes that she is praying not only for but with her child. Whenever it is possible she continues in the patterns of her family's life, sharing with friends, seeking out beauty in the world around her and spending time in church, joining in the services, and surrounding herself and her baby with an atmosphere of purity and holiness. Even if she has some natural fears, she looks forward in anticipation to the day of its birth, living each day joyfully and with a sense of awe. Without even realizing it, the baby absorbs her spirit of peace, joy and anticipation. The mother's spirit, and the spirit the child absorbs through her of its family and surroundings, gradually prepare it for its birth into this world.

When birth comes, the infant is ready and able to accept the sudden and enormous adjustment to being on its own in a new way. As it is quickly surrounded by warmth and attention, it recognizes that they come from the same sources with which it was acquainted during the long months just past. It is held, fed, cleaned, hugged and petted with enormous tolerance for its demanding needs.

When it is brought to the church, the sounds the baby hears clearly for the first time will already be familiar, and it may already sense however dimly that this is where its family finds the source for its own daily spirit of love, joy, peace and hope. It will forget the traumatic transition into this new stage of life. Full awareness of its surroundings, including the adoring family it finds itself part of, will grow with gradual delight. When it is confronted with pain and loss—illnesses and injuries, its own passionate, sinful reactions to almost everything, its own inability to achieve certain things it wants, perhaps a death in the immediate family, sin, failures and sorrows that touch those around it—the child learns that love and forgiveness are present and are the effective means of healing for itself and for the life of its family.

It becomes eager to explore the world afresh at each new level of its development. As the months and years go by, its family helps the child to grow in healthy ways, physically, emotionally and mentally. Parents and others introduce it to trusted teachers and guides outside the home and family, letting it exercise its body, mind and spirit and learn the joy of work and play. They teach when necessary but also listen and respect its need for time alone, allowing it to discover resources within itself that gradually bring greater and greater independence from them. Being loved without conditions, it instinctively respects and loves others and all of creation. It learns much without consciously being taught, including reverence for the actions and relationships of daily life. Spending its earliest months and years at home with the touching, the tastes, the sounds, scents and sights of a cultured atmosphere filled with literature, poetry, music and art and seeing that these reflect in turn the life and cult it knows in the church, it develops an innate awareness of the beauty of God's whole creation and begins to search for this wherever it finds itself. It recoils from experiences of abuse and learns that there is a right use for its anger and ability to resist. It is not tempted to use other people or things or situations as a substitute for living its own life. It understands from a very early age that its life, its family and surroundings are all a gift from God, and it learns to love Him most of all, gratefully reaching out to Him in the prayer and liturgical life its family shares.

When such people become adults, they realize with their families that they no longer need a child's care. The discovery may be gradual or as traumatic as their physical birth. Once again they are on their own in a new way. Yet as they accept their independence and the responsibility for providing for their own needs, they have a firm trust in God for all that lies ahead of them. They hear Him calling them to further life and work in love. They continue to recognize their families as the means He used to bring them to their present freedom. What they had first known as all-surrounding warmth and attention will have become the secure foundation of being loved, the solid step from which they set out to explore their new horizons.

As they delighted in their conceptions and births, their families delight in the developments of their adult lives, welcoming their new friends and loved ones, letting them widen the scope of their family of love. This love and the firm trust in God nurtured in them strengthen them in their own efforts to provide love and support for others. As the years go by, their families of origin remain among their closest friends, the ones who have shared their joys and sorrows, their experiences of growth and of loss from the very beginning. Their families also continue to respect and listen to them as well as sharing with them the continuing lessons they learn as adults. They share also their memories of those who are bound to them by ties of love, prayer, and kinship even though they may never have met. They grieve at times of separation yet know they are never separated in heart and spirit. When family and friends die, whether through old age, illness or tragedy, they are left with more than memories. Heaven opens to them through these people, and they discover a new way of knowing. They sense the presence of these loved ones and let them help as they graduallly free themselves from all they see that cannot last forever or provide them support into eternity. They prepare for the time of their physical death, seeing more and more that God in Christ is their all.

This was the life of Mary, raised in the home of her parents. It was the life of Jesus, raised in the family of Nazareth. It has been the life of many, such as the galaxy of saints we know now as "The Cappadocians," all members of the same 4th century circle of family and friends. May we sense the reality of the spiritual presence of such families in our lives, praying for us and giving us the support we need and the courage to forgive ourselves and our own families and friends for falling short of this perfection of Godly love.

19

Epilogue: Adam Cast Out of Paradise

I am Adam; I am Eve. I know the joy and the freedom of Paradise, but here I am sitting outside on the step, with the door closed behind me. And this is a direct result of my own choices.

I can't go back. I can't pretend this hasn't happened. I know the choices I have just made. And as much as I mourn for the beauty of paradise, I know that I am caught here pretty thoroughly. When I see things as vividly as I just saw them a few hours ago—when the serpent opened my eyes to the alternatives—even though I know the consequences now and realize that this seemingly clear vision of my alternatives was based on sheer illusion and was a lie, still, how seductive that vision of alternatives is!

Perhaps the serpent and I can work hard enough on those alternatives out here so that they will become what I want them to be, a form of life even more solid than the rarefied air of Paradise.

I've just learned that I have to work around the new fact of life my alternatives have created: death. That wasn't there before. How was I to know that when the pictures in my mind began to change and I saw that God was keeping me from something that would taste good and give me a good feeling, and that I could be "god" too and could set the rules as easily as He does... How could I know that my rules would bring death instead of the life His rules bring?

It isn't fair! I should be able to eat anything that I see and that looks good! Especially when there is someone there to assure me that denying myself is not necessary. What kind of a God is it, anyway, who would make up such rules? "Eat that fruit and you're dead." I'm not sure I can love such a God anymore.

He says that if I love Him, I'll keep His commandments. He just kicked me out of His place, so why should I love Him? I'll just forget Him and His rules and create my own reality. The serpent is out here with me, and he seems to be pretty sure of himself. If he can survive on his terms, I should be able to also.

I've got all this resentment and anger and it's going to be such hard work to maintain my life of alternatives, fighting against God all the way. It's just as well there is death. I don't have to go through this forever the way I would have had to if I'd passed up that fruit. I had to work pretty hard to keep up the garden of Paradise, though it sounds as if that part isn't going to be any easier out here. I don't like the way the animals are looking at me now, and all those beautiful plants seem to have turned into weeds. With death, though, it will all be over one of these days and I can rest. And in the meantime, I can enjoy my own rules.

But this is going to be hard. If I can think of all of this as a sort of game, I'll be fine. I'll make this life into a game of chance and have fun cheating. After all, I'm going to have to die anyway—why not enjoy myself on the way? There are so many things I can see that I enjoy, not just eating but also using and doing. Yet God's rules say that the way I'm going about this brings even more death. I have to work this out.

There is a problem here. I've heard that God has a real war going on with this serpent. He knows the serpent is sitting out here with me helping me think all these thoughts. What if He figures out a way to leave His perfect world and sit out here, too? It would be pretty uncomfortable to have Him around here. The serpent and I are setting up a whole alternative universe, and we should at least be allowed to play with it until we die. God kicked us out of His super-pure environment—I guess He felt He was too good for us and we'd just mess up His pretty arrangements. Well, now He can just leave us alone. We're adults. We can make our own decisions and live with the consequences. That death we've caused isn't such a bad thing after all, since we don't have to live with those consequences forever.

I'm having a pretty hard time. I've been living out here for awhile and now there are a lot of other people just like me in this world. Even I can see that this place isn't at all like paradise. My rules seem to run into trouble everywhere. All of us out here keep making decisions so we can continue to have our alternatives to God's way. I don't like the consequences of the other people's decisions. I'm willing to die for my own reasons, but why should I have to suffer for what some other stupid person does? It isn't fair. I need to work harder on my alternatives so they are stronger than other people's and then they won't be able to touch me. I'll ignore them or move away from them or find some other way to get rid of them if they won't follow my rules. After all, that's what God did to me, isn't it? I can even kill them if there is no other way.

I had a dream the other night. In my dream, God finally got out here in a way that I would never have imagined before. He managed to take on this flesh He gave me from one of my great-granddaughters. In my dream, it seemed that He had to live in this place just as I do. He had to face the results of everyone else's alternatives and have the serpent play games with His thoughts, too. He could make His flesh anything He wanted to, since He's kept that secret. He could have ruled every one of us and forced us to live here the way He wanted us to, since He could have been as powerful as He chose.

He did a very strange thing in my dream. He didn't even try to beat us at our own game. He picked the most vulnerable position possible. Instead of avoiding us, or putting up defenses so we couldn't touch Him, He spent all His time with us—wanted to get as close to us as He could. He kept talking about love, and the opposite of my own feelings of anger and resentment. He kept saying that forgiveness is the key. And He seemed to mean it. I knew Who He was, because once in my dream He blew His cover and let that glorious light of Paradise shine through when He went up a mountain with some disciples. But there was no other minute that seemed to make Him different from any of the rest of us.

My dream became like a nightmare toward the end. He could have done all the things I do to keep this life from getting too serious. He could have made it a game. Instead, He brought out the worst in us—really forced us to be as mean and cruel and resentful as we could be. He took away the atmosphere of niceness we've created out here to make up for that super-pure goodness and beauty of His we left behind in Paradise.

So we did the only thing we could do to keep our world going out here—after all, He's the one who made that rule about death—We killed Him.

But it's the last part of my dream that keeps bothering me. Death was supposed to end it for Him and for us, but it didn't. It seemed we killed His body, but we couldn't kill *Him*. He even managed to come back with the body we killed. It had that same Paradise glory it had had for that brief time on the mountain. And then I heard in my dream that because we couldn't kill Him that way, death won't be final for us either, since we are exactly like Him in every way except for all that goodness and love. Worse than that, I will be living on His terms again and I won't be able to continue to play all my games. The fun will be gone.

When I woke from my dream, the serpent came over to reassure me at once. It wasn't real. Even if something like that could happen, we still have our alternatives. I can keep being resentful for having to be out here going through all this and I can continue to avoid God, even if He comes to me showing me how much He understands and loves since He has been out here Himself. I can continue to prefer my games and my rules. The serpent pointed out that he himself is going to do that, and I can join him. We'll keep this life of alternatives going for eternity, just as we have it here. Only there won't be any death to end it. It will get worse and worse for eternity. All of us will be making up our own rules and no one else will obey them. We'll spend all our time destroying each other's dreams and creations. It will be hell.

How hard would it be to move away from this serpent? This God—He even has a name now—He let me call Him Jesus in my dream—what would happen if I tried to do it His way instead? What if I can learn to love and forgive? What if I begin to deny myself some of those alternatives I know will never make it in paradise?

It is going to be very, very hard. And I'm going to be as defenseless as He was here. All those noble things: laying down my life, my dreams and my plans because I want to help someone else? Learning to love someone else enough to do that? Even letting that someone else be anyone else?

Not picking and choosing which ones are worth it? He says there is no one who isn't worth it. It is tempting. He even says He will give me His own life so I will have the strength and the love and the power to do things His way.

I have to think about this. I realize now that I have a decision to make. I'm just not sure which way I really want to go.